First Edition, July 2020

DEDICATION

Jack Stanley here. Before I wrote this book, I looked through several existing "Kids Coding books." I found two common problems with them:

1) They were too difficult. Many of the explanations contained words that many kids (and adults) don't know. And,

2) They were boring.

Then it hit me – *what if I wrote a coding book for kids as a story?!* Meaning, it would contain characters and dialogue (spoken conversations). This would allow me to be quite imaginative. I then wrote this book and my genius business partner (Erik Gross) reviewed, edited and added his charm to it. It is Erik's and my dream that this book will end up in schools all over the world.

Even though I am technically a grown up, I never really grew up. I am the father of two wonderful children, and I have nieces and nephews. They are the primary source of my motivation.

This book is dedicated to them.

Jack C. Stanley,
July 2020

THE TECH ACADEMY

LEARNCODINGANYWHERE.COM ®

LEARN CODING BASICS
FOR KIDS, YOUNG ADULTS AND
PEOPLE WHO ARE YOUNG AT HEART
WITH

Written by: Jack C. Stanley and Erik D. Gross

Illustrations by: Afra Amin Orony, based on sketches by Jack C. Stanley

TABLE OF CONTENTS

Chapter One: Welcome, 7

Chapter Two: What is Coding?, 19

Chapter Three: What Do Snakes Have To Do With This?, 31

Chapter Four: Downloading and Installing Python, 37

Chapter Five: Math, 51

Chapter Six: Data in Programs, 57

Chapter Seven: Comparing Numbers, 63

Chapter Eight: Data Comparisons, 69

Chapter Nine: If, 75

Chapter Ten: Lists, 83

Chapter Eleven: Loopy, 95

Chapter Twelve: Dictionaries, 105

Chapter Thirteen: Functions, 111

Chapter Fourteen: Python Functions, 121

Chapter Fifteen: Input, 131

Chapter Sixteen: Rock, Paper, Scissors, 151

Chapter Seventeen: Hangman, 155

Epilogue: 161

Index: 165

Other Reading: 167

CHAPTER ONE
WELCOME

"Erik!" Jack yelled in excitement. "Someone is reading our book!"

"Well, that was our reason for writing it," Erik responded. "Let's introduce ourselves. I am Erik and-"

"And I am Jack!" Jack interrupted. "It's nice to meet you! Erik and I have a school called The Tech Academy."

Jack   **Erik**

"*Tech* is short for technology," Jack continued, "and *Academy* is just another word for school. *Technology* means to use the things you know to solve problems and to make life easier."

"So, you're saying toilet paper is technology?" Erik asked.

"Well, not exactly. I mean, kind of, it-"

"Because it certainly makes my life easier!"

"Very funny, Erik. What I was trying to tell our wonderful reader is that the things that we use to do work for us are technology."

"Like toilet paper!"

"Enough with the toilet paper," Jack demanded. "What I mean is that technology is machines and the things we tell machines to do."

"Ah, and machines are things made by people to get work done," Erik explained. "Machines do actions for people to save them time and to get things done faster. They're usually made out of wood, plastic or metal. Normally they have some parts that move and some parts that don't – sometimes they have no moving parts at all! Machines receive some kind of energy (like electricity or gas) that they use to do their work. One of the things that makes people different from animals is their ability to create powerful machines."

"So, cars, ovens and televisions are machines?" Jack wondered.

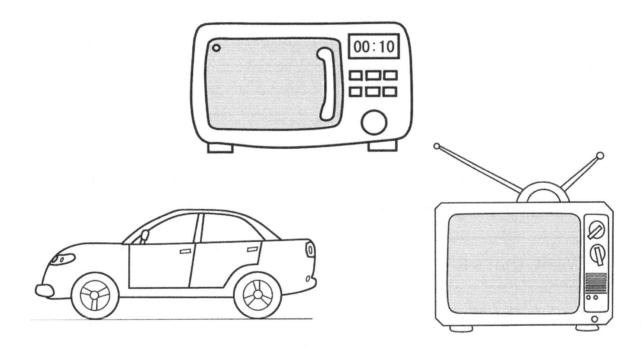

"Yep!" Erik replied. "The most popular machine in the world right now is computers."

"Okay, Erik, don't be a nerd," Jack teased.

"I am proud to be a nerd!"

"Okay, okay. I take it back. Now why are you saying computers are more popular than any other machines? Don't more people have cars or refrigerators?"

"Well, actually, nowadays almost every machine has a computer inside it – most phones, televisions, airplanes, cars and refrigerators included! Oh, I just realized, we haven't really said what a computer is exactly."

"That's easy. A computer is a machine that computes. Just like a baker is someone who bakes, a gamer is someone who plays games-"

"Jack! What does *compute* mean?"

"It's very, very, very difficult to understand. So, get ready... Compute means figuring out the answer to a problem."

"Wait, that's it?"

"Well, technically it's solving problems with numbers."

"So, math is computing?"

"Yep!"

"So," Erik began, "computers are machines that compute. They do things with numbers."

"Yes," Jack agreed, "they are machines that work with data. Data is just another word for information – facts and knowledge about things. Erik, why don't you tell our amazing reader how computers work?"

"I thought you'd never ask!" Erik responded excitedly. "It could take a whole book to describe that exactly. In fact, that's why we wrote a different book called *You Are Not Stupid – Computers and Technology Simplified –* available now for purchase on Amazon!"

"Erik!" Jack butted in. "Stop trying to sell other books!"

"Sorry, it's an old habit," Erik apologized. "Did you know I used to sell sunglasses all around the world?"

Jack tapped his foot impatiently.

"So, as I was saying," Erik chuckled nervously, "computers are machines that use electricity to operate (do things). They deal with data (information). Computers have several parts that electricity passes through. Computers are not alive – they are just a tool, like a lawnmower or a hammer. We use them to do things for us. Computers simply follow instructions – which are commands that tell them what to do."

"Erik!" Jack shouted. "Take those sunglasses off! We are inside!" With a sly smile, Erik removed his sunglasses and put his glasses back on. "Now," Jack continued, "there are a couple other things about computers that I would like to add:

"1. *Automatic* means that a machine can do something by itself. *Automate* means to make something automatic. Machines that automate things do those things on their own. **Computers automate various actions.** Meaning, they can do things without you being involved. For example, your computer automatically says what time it is and automatically turns the screen off when it hasn't been used for a while. Keep in mind that these automatic actions were originally designed (created) by a person.

"2. **Computers process data.** *Process* means to handle something according to certain rules. When a computer displays the word 'processing,' it is saying, 'Hold on while I perform some actions according to certain rules and steps built into me.' *Processing* refers to 'doing things with data.' Loading up and showing a video on your computer is an example of 'processing data.' When data is being processed by a computer, you sometimes see this 'progress bar' (a picture that shows how far along something is):"

Processing...

"Took you long enough to explain that," Erik yawned. "Want to hear a fun fact?"

"I'm pretty sure you're going to tell it to me no matter what," Jack replied.

"Okay! Have you ever seen this?"

"Yeah," Jack answered. "It's like a spinning circle that shows up when data is being processed."

"Yep!" Erik acknowledged. "When information is being handled by a computer the spinny circle is shown but do you know what it's called?"

"Ummmm... a spinny thingy?"

"Good guess, but no. It's called a *throbber* because when they first came out, they would go between getting bigger and smaller. They throbbed!"

"Erik, you're making my head throb. Let's move on..."

"Alright, do you know what it's called when we *put* data *in* to a computer?"

"Is this a guessing game or a book? It's called input – when you input data, you're putting data inside the computer."

"Exactly! What about when you take information out of the computer?"

"Ummmm... Takeout? Just kidding, it's called *output*. But why does all this matter, Erik?"

"I'm getting there. Input has two meanings:

"1. As a thing, it is the data put into a computer,

"2. As an action, it means to put data into a computer.

Output means the opposite."

"Yeah, yeah, we get it. So, what's the point?"

"The point is that computers work this way:

"1)   They take data in. Meaning, information or instructions is input into the computer – usually by a person.

"2)   They process that data. This means they perform actions with the data that was input.

"3)   Then they send data out. Such as by displaying (showing) the data on your computer screen or printing the data with a printer. Meaning, the output is what you see on the screen or paper."

INPUT   PROCESS   OUTPUT

"That's pretty cool," Jack admitted. "When you put it that simply, I guess computers are pretty basic. So, remember how I was talking about technology earlier – things you use to complete work faster and make life easier? Well, computers are technology. In fact, the subjects are so similar that the two words ('computers' and 'tech') sometimes mean the same thing! For example, because of the fact that many machines contain computers, most 'tech news' is really 'computer news.' Now, Erik, I have a serious question. What do spiders do on computers?"

"I don't know," Erik answered, "what?"

"Make websites!"

Erik laughed so loud that Jack had to plug his ears. "Jack," Erik began, "I think this chapter is getting a little long."

"I agree," Jack responded. "Let's end this chapter and then talk about what coding is!"

CHAPTER TWO
WHAT IS CODING?

Jack and Erik stood inside the The Tech Academy, wishing they were as cool as the person reading this book.

"Okay, Jack," Erik started, "what is coding?"

"I am glad you asked," Jack responded, "*coding* just means to put instructions (commands) into a computer."

"So, when I tell my computer to play a video, I'm coding?"

"Well, no. I guess to explain this, I will need to say what a program is."

"Allow me!" Erik cut in. "Programs are instructions, typed into a computer by people, that make the computer do certain things. Behind every action a computer can take, there's a program."

"Totally," Jack agreed, "here are some examples of programs:

- "Microsoft Word – which is a program that allows you to type things.

- "Google Chrome – a program that helps you search the internet.

- "Minecraft – a program that you've probably played!

"That's right, computer games are programs! And when you install a program on your computer, that just means you're putting the program on the computer so it can be used. Just like if you say, 'I installed a door,' you mean that you put a door on your house."

"I have another fun fact!" Erik blurted out.

Jack rolled his eyes.

"Programs are also called applications (apps for short) and software," Erik explained. "Guess what the opposite of software (programs) is?"

"Toughware?" Jack guessed.

Erik giggled. "Nope! Hardware! Get it? *Soft*ware and *hard*ware are opposites."

"I get it! Hardware is the physical parts of a computer – the parts that you can touch. *Hard* literally means *solid* or *able to be touched*. *Ware* is *something created that can be sold or used*. For example, *teaware* refers to everything you can use for drinking tea – like tea cups, teapots and bags of tea. The computer screen, mouse, printer and keyboard are all examples of hardware."

"So, again," Erik stated as he stood in front of Jack, "software is computer programs – instructions that tell a computer what to do. Software is made by people to make the computer do certain things and to give certain output (information put out). The software is the instructions, while hardware follows the instructions."

"Back to what this has to do with coding," Jack said, pushing Erik out of the way, "*coding* means to create computer programs. People that create programs (software and apps) are called coders. They're also called software developers or computer programmers. A developer is someone who makes something."

"I'm confused..." Erik whined. "So many of these words mean the same thing. An app is a program and is software. A computer programmer, is a coder, is a software developer, is a-"

"Oh my dear silly Erik, it's not confusing," Jack explained. "Having lots of names for the same thing is very common in English. For example, *huge*, *giant* and *gigantic* all mean the same thing."

"Hey! Stop talking about my belly!" Erik covered his stomach with both hands. "Moving on... *Code* can be an action – making computer programs by writing special instructions into a computer. It can also be a thing. *Code* is the actual instructions. For example, this code:

```
Show Picture (Cat)
```

"And it could make your computer show a picture of a cat."

"Now that is a cute cat," Jack stated.

"You would write this code inside a special program called an-" Erik started.

"Hold on," Jack cut in, "you're about to say three really big words."

"I know, I know. But I didn't choose the name for this thing! The reader needs to know what it's called."

Jack thought about it and then nodded in agreement.

"The program that coders use to write their code in is called an *Integrated Development Environment*."

Jack yawned.

"*Integrate* means to combine things together," Erik went on. "For example, if you integrate red and blue, you get purple. The program you use to write your code in is *integrated* because there are many different things it can do that are brought together in one place."

"Okay, I guess that makes sense," Jack admitted. "And the development part refers to making programs – like software development."

"That's right. *Environment* refers to a place where you can live or work. So, when we put it all together, an Integrated Development Environment is simply the program that you write your code in. It is software that helps you make software."

"I don't like saying Integrated Development Environment – it's too complicated. Can I just call it an IDE?"

"Sure thing. In fact, that's what most professionals call it."

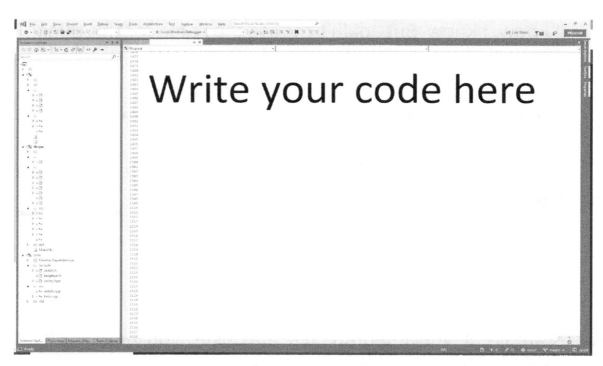

This is an IDE

"So, the IDE is the program where we type the instructions that make programs," Jack repeated. "These programs are written using programming languages."

"Wait," Erik interrupted, "computers speak languages? Like Spanish or Chinese?"

"First off, Chinese people mostly speak Mandarin, not 'Chinese.' Second of all, to answer your question, yes, just like people speak lots of languages, computers have their own languages that they can 'understand.' These programming languages are the words we use to write our programs. There are many different programming languages. Just like hammers and ladders have different uses, each programming language has a different use. For example, some programming languages were designed mainly to improve websites, while others were made for creating computer games. The instructions used in programming languages are code. For example, to have a computer show the word 'Hello!' using Python (the *very* popular programming language you will learn in this book), the code is written as:"

```
print("Hello!")
```

"When someone says 'program a computer' or 'do some coding,'" Jack continued, "they're saying, 'Write a set of instructions into a computer, using a programming language, that will result in specific actions being performed when that set of instructions is done.' Again, a computer programmer is a person that does computer programming (writes code that makes programs)."

"So," Erik started, "do you know what it's called when you make your code go?"

"Go where?" Jack asked.

"I mean, you type some code and then you make it do what you wanted it to do. When computers perform actions, like when they do things, we call this 'executing' or 'running.'"

"Executing your code! Why would we kill it?"

"No, again, *execute* means to make the computer do things. Like you could *execute* an instruction by pressing Enter on your keyboard."

"Okay, but what is our code running away from?"

"Huh?"

"You said that code can run?"

"Oh, it doesn't mean that. *Run* means the same thing as *execute*. For example, you can *run* a search on the internet by clicking the search button. "

"Ah, now I remember. Inside our IDE (the program we will use to write our code) there is a button we can press to run (execute) our code – this makes the code go – it makes the code take action!"

"Erik," Jack began, "I hate it when chapters go on and on. Can we talk about the snake now?"

"What snake?" Erik asked in confusion.

"Python. See, I'm holding one right now. You said this book was about pythons."

"Jack!" squealed Erik. "Weren't you paying attention earlier when I said that Python was a popular computer programming language? Get rid of that snake!"

"Oops!" Jack said, embarrassed. "Okay, let's talk about what Python is in the next chapter – and we need to hurry, because I'm pretty sure the reader wants to write some code soon! But first, I need to make a quick return at the pet store..."

CHAPTER THREE
WHAT DO SNAKES HAVE TO DO WITH THIS?

"Erik, who is this guy?" Jack said while holding a picture.

"That's Guido van Rossum," Erik answered, "the guy that created the programming language Python."

"Oh man, he must be a really smart guy if he created an entire programming language!" Jack announced. "So, why did he call it Python? Does he love snakes?"

"Actually, it's named after an old television show from the 1960s and 1970s. The show was called 'Monty Python' and it was really funny. Guido was a big fan!"

(Monty Python actors)

"Erik, you're so old..." Jack said. "So, why are we using Python in this book?"

"Simple," Erik started, "because many of the words used in Python are English words! For example, to add numbers in Python we write this code:

1 + 2

"Python will return (give back to us):

3

"Just like how we would write it in English!"

"That's right," Jack remembered. "Python is a great way to learn coding because it is so similar to what we're used to! So, to use Python we have to download it. Do you know what *downloading* means?"

"Yes, but why don't you say it?" Erik looked a little nervous and uncertain.

"*Download* just means you're taking something online (from the internet) and putting it on your computer. The internet is just a way to share information between computers. For example, if you download a video, you are having your computer pull the video's data from the internet (from other computers) and save that data on your computer so you can watch it later. So, Erik, what's the opposite of *download*?"

"Highload?"

"Close, but no. The opposite of *down*load is *up*load. When you upload something, you are moving it from your computer to the internet. Like you could upload a video that you recorded to YouTube and then you could be famous! In the picture below, the large computers at the top are the 'internet' – powerful computers used to share information."

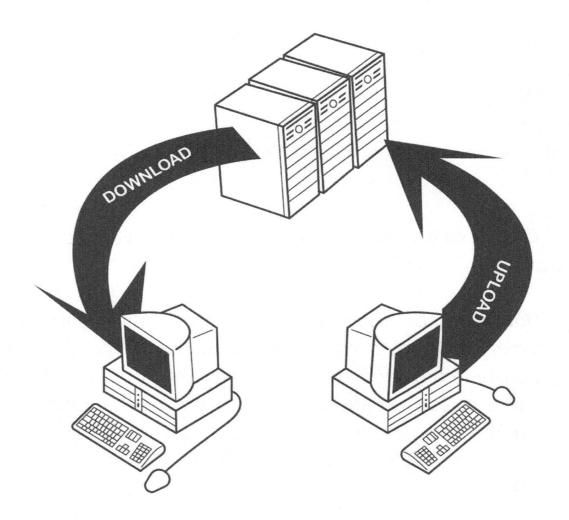

"Hold on," Erik said in excitement, "I can upload my videos and become famous?"

"Well, I mean, it's possible but not likely-"

"Focus, Erik, focus," Jack instructed, "you can upload your singing and dancing videos later. We have been talking for three chapters and the reader hasn't been able to write any code yet. I say we get started!"

"Yes!" Erik agreed. "So, what's the first step?"

"Well," Jack began, "the first step is to download (take from the internet) and install (put on our computer) Python."

"That sounds hard."

"Don't worry Erik, we can get through it, together!"

"You're right," Erik agreed happily. "But can we do it in the next chapter? There's a certain video of me singing Taylor Swift that I just have to upload. The world *needs* to see my new dance move! I call it 'The Gross-Gross'!"

"Just so the reader knows, Gross is Erik's last name. But now that I've seen him dance, I think the name of his dance might have two meanings..."

CHAPTER FOUR
DOWNLOADING AND INSTALLING PYTHON

"Okay, Erik," Jack started, "I watched your video and just finished washing my eyes. Let's get to work."

"Haters are going to hate," Erik said, "and I'm just going to shake it off!"

"The first step to adding Python to your computer is to go here on the internet:

`python.org`

"Then click Downloads and select the newest version (type) of Python (in the picture below, you would click on the rectangle that says Python 3.8.3 – it doesn't matter if the version number on your screen is different):

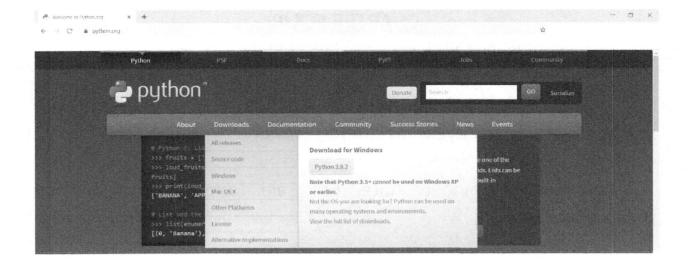

"After you click on the newest version of Python, you should see a little rectangle in the bottom of your screen that looks something like this:

"If you don't see it there, check in your computer's Downloads folder."

"Click on the rectangle that says 'python...' on the bottom of your screen or the file named 'python...' inside your Downloads folder. When it opens, click 'Install Now.'"

"When it asks you, 'Are you sure?' click Yes. Then when you see 'Setup was successful,' you can click 'Close.' Now don't worry if the pictures you see and the names and numbers on your screen are slightly different than our pictures – technology changes all the time. All that's important here is that you successfully download and install Python, which I am sure you did!"

"We made it!" Erik cheered.

"Yes, we did!" Jack agreed. "So, how do we write code?"

"Well, remember that long name 'Integrated Development Environment' – the program you use to write programs in?"

"Ah, yes. The I-D-E."

"Yep! We need to open Python's IDE. The Python IDE is named 'IDLE.' This stands for 'Integrated Development and Learning Environment.' Remember how I told you that the creator of Python, Guido van Rossum, named this language after the TV show Monty Python? Well, I think the name IDLE was probably chosen partly to honor Eric Idle, one of the actors from the Monty Python TV show."

"Erik, you certainly love your random facts! So, IDLE is what we will use to write our Python code. There are two parts to IDLE:

"1) **Shell.** This is a program that lets you control your computer by writing commands. It is called a shell because it is the part in between the coder and their computer – like a crab shell is the part between the crab and the outside world. The Python shell looks something like this:

"2) **Text editor.** Text is characters (letters, numbers and symbols).

A B C	1 2 3	! # ?
(letters)	(numbers)	(symbols)

Edit means to change something written. A text editor is a program that you use to write and edit text. It can also be used to write code! Python's text editor looks like this:"

"Now, Erik, can we please, please, please write some code?" Jack begged.

"Certainly!" Erik acknowledged. "Let's open up IDLE and type-"

"Hold on, my friend," Jack interrupted. "How do we open IDLE?"

"Sorry, I am just so excited that we are finally going to write code. There are lots of ways we can open IDLE but my favorite way is to go to the search bar at the bottom of my screen."

"Then I type IDLE and click on it!"

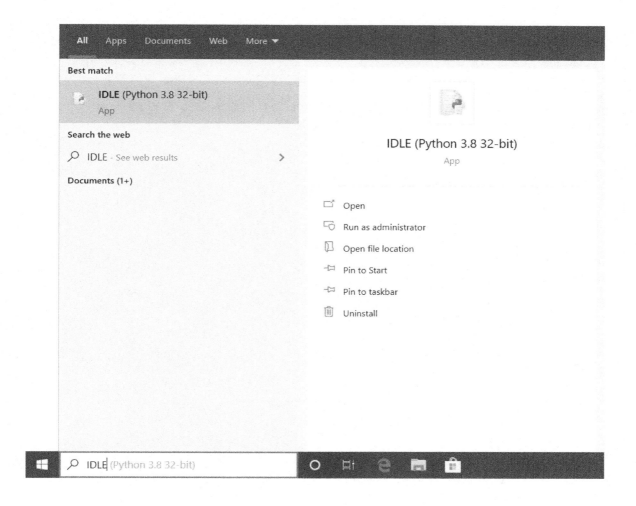

"Now you should see the shell!"

```
Python 3.8.3 Shell                                          —    □    ×
File  Edit  Shell  Debug  Options  Window  Help
Python 3.8.3 (tags/v3.8.3:6f8c832, May 13 2020, 22:20:19) [MSC v.1925 32 bit (In
tel)] on win32
Type "help", "copyright", "credits" or "license()" for more information.
>>> |


                                                                      Ln: 3  Col: 4
```

"Cowabunga!" Jack yelled.

"Let's make it bigger by maximizing the shell," Erik said. "You do this by clicking the square in the top right corner. *Maximize* just means to make something it's biggest size."

Click here

"Okay, done," Jack stated. "Reader, you should just keep it maximized throughout the whole book. So, this shell is where we write our code?"

"Yes!" Erik answered.

"What do all those random words and numbers at the top mean?"

"Oh, you don't need to worry about all that – just ignore them. What does matter are the >>>. The >>> show us where to type our code. So, let's make the computer return (say something back) a piece of data. The first thing that people usually make computers say when learning to code is 'Hello, World.'"

"Hello, world? I don't get it."

"I think they're having the computer 'introduce' itself to the world or something."

"Oh, I see. I'd like to make it more exciting than that... Let's make the computer say, 'Hey there big, wonderful, happy, amazing, awesome planet Earth!!!!!!' Type this inside IDLE:"

```
>>> print("Hey there big, wonderful, happy,
amazing, awesome planet Earth!!!!!!")
```

"Keep all the text on one line," Erik directed. "In fact, you should always keep each single command on one line from here forward unless we tell you otherwise."

"Exactly," Jack agreed. "Now press enter. Yay! You made the computer print something on the screen! If you had an error, make sure that you included all of the characters (letters and symbols). For example, if you leave off a quotation mark, parentheses or even if you write print with a capital p (Print) – your code won't run! *You have to write code exactly like we have it in the book*."

"What?" Erik asked. "You're saying one wrong thing, like a typo, makes it so that your code won't work?"

"Yeah," Jack replied. "It can be a little annoying but those are the rules."

"So, to print something, I type print, followed by parentheses, then a quotation mark, then the text I want to print, then another quotation mark, and finally another parenthesis?"

"Yep! Let me show you why it's important to follow the rules of programming language exactly. Type this inside of IDLE:"

```
>>> print(Hey there big, wonderful, happy,
amazing, awesome planet Earth!!!!!!)
```

"Can I just go back and change my earlier code?" Erik asked.

"Nope," Jack answered. "In the shell, you can't edit the code you ran earlier – you have to write new code."

"Ah, I see."

"Okay," Jack began, "in the code we just wrote, we took out the quotation marks. If you haven't already pressed enter, do so now. There is an error! Actually, it says 'SyntaxError.' What the heck is *syntax*, Erik?"

"I know that word sounds complicated – but all that syntax is, is the rules for a programming language," Erik explained. "For example, including parentheses and quotation marks is part of the syntax for printing things in Python. A syntax error means that we broke the rules and didn't type our code correctly."

"Interesting. Now, just so you know, you can also print things by surrounding your text with apostrophes. Type this inside IDLE:"

```
>>> print('Jack and Erik are the best')
```

"Press enter," Jack directed. "And thank you for saying we are the best!"

"Now that's some good code," Erik stated. "So, Jack, do you know what the text that the computer displays is called?"

"You mean, 'Jack and Erik are the best!'?"

"Yes, that."

"It's called the truth!"

"Well, yes. But technically, that text is called a *string*."

"What does sewing have to do with this?" Jack asked.

"Nothing," Erik answered. "Jack, put that string away! You can sew a new pair of underwear later! In coding, a *string* is the word we use to say that we have one or more characters. Remember, characters are letters, numbers and symbols. It's called a string because the characters are strung together (connected). The two strings that you printed in this chapter were:

```
"1)  Hey there big, wonderful, happy, amazing, awesome
     planet Earth!!!!!!
```

And

```
"2)  Jack and Erik are the best!
```

"Now, let's give our intelligent reader a challenge," Erik stated. "Reader, we challenge you to do this in IDLE:"

```
● Print a string of your own.
```

After the reader successfully printed their own string, Erik and Jack shouted, "Good job!"

"Hey, Jack," Erik said, "let's do some math now."

"But I want to keep writing code in Python..." Jack complained.

"That's what I mean! We can do math with Python. I'll show you in the next chapter."

CHAPTER FIVE
MATH

Erik stood in front of a nearly empty classroom talking to no one but the reader and Jack. He was wearing suspenders and his favorite pair of dark pink glasses.

"Welcome, class!" Erik began a little too excitedly. "Today we are going to talk about math. *Math* is short for *mathematics*. The word *mathematics* basically means 'to do things with numbers and shapes.' It includes the study of numbers and what we can do with them. In math-"

"Ooh, ooh!" Jack cried out raising his hand.

"Yes, student."

"Did you know that the word *mathematics* comes from the very old words *mathematike*, which meant 'art,' and *manthanein*, which meant 'learn'?"

"Jack! I'm the one wearing suspenders, which means I'm the one teaching this class. Now, as I was saying: in math, an *operator* is a symbol used when doing a math problem. These are all operators:
- $+$ (add),
- $-$ (subtract),
- $\div$ (divide), and
- $\times$ (multiply)

"We use these operators to do math," Erik stated.

"Yes, now I remember," Jack said. "Alright, our incredible reader: open up IDLE and type this code:"

```
>>> 1 + 1
```

"Press enter," Jack instructed.

"The answer is 3!" Erik announced.

"Uh, Erik..." Jack started.

"Just kidding," Erik said blushing. "You should see 2."

"You can also subtract," Jack stated. "Write this code in IDLE:"

```
>>> 9 - 4
```

"Press enter," Jack directed. "Good job! Now, to multiply, we don't write X, we use this symbol *," Jack explained. "This little star is called an asterisk."

"An asteroid?" Erik asked.

"No, asterisk."

"An amphibian?"

"Never mind," Jack sighed. "So, to do multiplication, write this code in IDLE:"

```
>>> 5 * 3
```

"Press enter," Jack said. "You got 15!"

"That's cool," Erik said. "To divide, we use a forward slash /. It's called a forward slash because it is a mark that looks like it's leaning forward in the sentence, since words go from left to right in English. Did you know there are languages where the words are written from right to left – like Arabic and Hebrew?"

"Okay Erik – now you're being a word nerd..."

"*Arabic* is a language spoken in many countries – including Saudi Arabia. And *Hebrew* is the language spoken by Hebrews – people who live in Israel and Palestine or their family, and some people who are Jewish."

"Can we get back to dividing numbers please?", pleaded Jack.

"Okay, fine. Write this code in IDLE:"

```
>>>20 / 2
```

"We just wrote twenty divided by two," Erik explained. "Press enter. We got 10!"

"That's awesome!" Jack announced. "Erik, did you know that you can also use the plus sign to connect strings (text)? This is called *concatenating strings*. *Concatenate* is just a fancy word for connecting things together."

"Connecticut?" Erik asked.

"No, concatenate."

"Co-"

"Erik, I'm not doing this again... If you concatenate your cell phone to the cell phone charger, it means you connect the cell phone to the charger and your cell phone is now charging. In coding, if you concatenate the string 'like' with the string 'able,' you would get the string 'likeable.' To see this, write this code in IDLE:"

```
>>> print('Jack ' + 'and Erik ' + 'are having
fun!')
```

"Press enter," Jack instructed. "We concatenated three strings! Which, again, is a fancy way of saying that we joined together these three groups of words:

"1. Jack

"2. and Erik

"3. are having fun!"

"And now, dear reader," Erik said as he looked right at you with intensity, "it's time for a challenge. Do this in IDLE:"

- `Add two numbers,`
- `Subtract two numbers,`
- `Divide two numbers,`
- `Multiply two numbers, and`
- `Concatenate two strings.`

Once you completed the challenge, Erik and Jack both did backflips at the same time and shouted, "You did it!" Erik landed on his feet and Jack landed on his head.

"I feel like my brain is bigger!" Erik yelled. "So, Jack, what's next?"

"Well, let's turn the page and find out!" Jack answered while he rubbed the top of his head.

CHAPTER SIX
DATA IN PROGRAMS

Erik and Jack sat on a bench, staring at the sunset and dreaming about what it would be like to be as smart as you.

"Well, Erik," Jack said, "I just don't think we could ever be that intelligent."

"You're right," Erik agreed, "the reader is just too smart. Let's go back to the school and write some code." They happily skipped down the street and walked back into the best school in the world: The Tech Academy.

"Okay, now it's time to learn a new word," Erik said. "The word is *vary*."

"Like, Jack is *vary* handsome?" Jack joked.

"No, not *very*, *vary*. They sound the same but they're not the same word. *Vary* means *to change*. When something varies, it becomes different. Like the weather – it varies depending on the season – sometimes it's hot, sometimes it's cold."

"I try not to vary very much."

"Vary funny... Now when you add the word 'able' to the end of something, it means that that thing is able to do something – it can be done. For example, if something is eatable, you can eat it – or if something is breakable, it can be broken."

"So what?"

"When you combine (put together) the words *vary* and *able*, you get the word *variable*. When something is variable, it means it can change – it is able to change. And so, variables are just things that can change."

"So, like a person's hair or the length of your fingernails? These are both variables?"

"Sure, they can change. When we talk about variables in coding, we are talking about data we use in a program that can be changed. For example, a person's name or a color could be variables. There are two parts of variables:

"1. The name. Also called an identifier – something used to identify (say what something is). The variable's name is used to identify an exact piece of data.

"2. The value. *Value* means *amount* or *type*. The value part of a variable shows the data we need to keep track of."

"Erik, you're confusing me."

"Okay, allow me to explain this more. We use an equal sign to assign (give) a value to the name of a variable, like this:"

```
Cat = Brown
```

"We are telling the computer that the cat (name) is brown (value). This is a variable. Now that I've explained that, let's create a variable. Open up IDLE and write this code:"

```
>>> Jack = 'Funny'
```

"Press enter," Erik directed.

"Why, thank you, Erik," Jack said. "But nothing happened."

"Oh, something happened. The computer stored (saved) that variable, you just can't see it. The variable name is *Jack*, and its value is the string (connected characters) *Funny*. To see it, type this code in IDLE:"

```
>>> print(Jack)
```

"Press enter," Erik instructed.

"Whoa!" Jack exclaimed. "How does that work?"

"Well," Erik began, "The computer associates (connects) the name *Jack* with the value *Funny* – it kind of thinks these are the same thing in a way. But now let me show you why it's called a variable (something that can change). Type this code in IDLE and press enter after each line:"

```
>>> Jack = 'Silly'
>>> print(Jack)
```

"Hey!" Jack argued.

"We changed the variable!" Erik explained. "It now prints *Silly* instead of *Funny*."

"Oh, so that's why it's a variable – it can vary (change)," Jack said.

"Exactamundo!" Erik proclaimed. "Now, I want you to try something. Type this code in IDLE:"

```
>>> print(jack)
```

"Here we wrote Jack with a lowercase j," Erik explained. "Now press enter. It didn't work! This goes back to that earlier word we used, *syntax* (the rules of a programming language). One of the rules in Python is to use consistent (always the same) capitalization."

"Makes sense!" Jack exclaimed. "We can also do math with variables. Write this code in IDLE and press enter after each line:"

```
>>> Jack = 10
>>> Erik = 20
>>> Jack + Erik
```

"Whoa!" Erik yelled. "You turned our names into numbers!"

"Yep!" Jack agreed. "Technically, what we did here is assigned (created) two variables:

"1. Jack (the variable name), 10 (the variable value), and

"2. Erik (name), 20 (value).

"Then we added these variables together!" Jack explained.

"Awesome!" Erik shouted. "Okay, our dearest friend, the reader of this book, the champion of the centuries, the mermaid in the sky, the-"

"I think they get it, Erik."

"Okay, okay, here is your challenge. Open IDLE and do the following:"

- Create your own variable,
- Print your variable,
- Create two variables and add them together, and
- Create two variables and subtract one from the other.

Jack and Erik stared in awe as the reader did a better job at this challenge than either of them could've ever hoped for. Once you finished, they hugged each other, crying.

Jack wiped the tears off of his eyes and said, "It's just so amazing..."

Erik blinked away his tears and said, "In the next chapter, we will go over how to compare things in Python."

CHAPTER SEVEN
COMPARING NUMBERS

Jack threw his phone down in frustration. "What is it, old friend?" Erik asked.

"I just Googled how to become as good looking as the person reading this book," Jack replied, "and it's just not possible!"

"Well, if you can't do it, I certainly have no hope."

"Thanks, grandpa Erik."

"I'm not your grandpa!"

"I know, but you are a grandpa – you have grandchildren."

"Ahem," Erik cleared his throat nervously and then chuckled. "My age has nothing to do with this book. And if I *am* a grandpa (not saying I am) I am the coolest grandpa in the world. Now then, let's look at how to compare numbers in Python. This is done by using these symbols:
> which mean more than
< which means less than"

"Those look like little mouths turned to the side," Jack stated. "Like tiny pacmen, wanting to eat something."

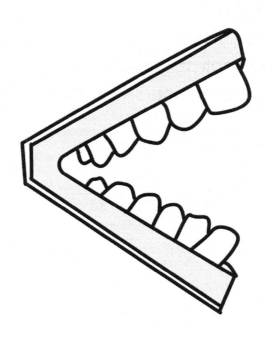

"I mean, I guess you could look at it that way," Erik answered. "The 'mouth' always points toward the bigger number. Like this: 10 > 4 (this means ten is bigger than four) or 5 < 12 (this means five is smaller than twelve)."

"Cool!" Jack announced.

"In Python," Erik continued, "when we compare numbers, the computer either tells us True or False. For example, this is True: 12 < 35 (twelve *is* less than thirtyfive)

"But this is False: 16 > 32 (sixteen is *not* more than thirtytwo)

"This is easier to understand by writing code. Write this code in IDLE:"

```
>>> 195 > 57
```

"Press enter," Erik instructed. "That's True! Because 195 is a bigger number than 57. Now write this code in IDLE:"

```
>>> 35 > 87
```

"Press enter," Erik said. "That's False! Okay, now let's try the lesser than sign (<). Write this code in IDLE:"

```
>>> 45 < 70
```

"Press enter," Erik commanded. "That's True!

```
>>> 311 < 182
```

"Press enter," Erik directed. "That's False!"

"Okay," Jack said, "Now let's get fancier. Write this code in IDLE and press enter after each line:"

```
>>> Erik = 100
>>> Jack = 50
>>> Erik > Jack
```

"Hey!" Erik yelled, "You just said 'Erik is bigger than Jack!' I'm on a diet!"

"But you're eating a doughnut right now!" Jack replied.

"Yeah, I'm on the doughnut diet!"

"I don't think that's a thing…" Jack disagreed. "Anyways, did you know that < and > are actually operators (symbols or words used to perform actions on numbers or compare things)? Alright, for our genius reader, we have another challenge. Do the following in IDLE:"

- Get the computer to return True by using the > operator,
- Return False using the > operator,
- Get the computer to return True by using the < operator,
- Return False using the < operator, and
- Assign (create) two variables as numbers, and then compare them using either the < or > operator.

As the reader worked on the challenge, Erik searched for Jack. He couldn't find him anywhere. Erik looked through the whole school and, finally, decided to check the roof. When he climbed on the roof, he found Jack staring at a beautiful rainbow.

"What's wrong, Jack?" Erik asked.

"Nothing, Erik the grandpa," Jack answered. "Absolutely nothing. I was just looking at this rainbow – the most beautiful rainbow I have ever seen and I realized something. The way the reader of this book completed our challenge was more beautiful than the beautifulist rainbow. I am just… amazed…"

Erik stood next to Jack and gazed at the rainbow in total agreement.

"In the next chapter," Jack said, "we should go over other ways we can make comparisons with Python."

"Sounds good, Jack. Let's head back down into the school."

CHAPTER EIGHT
DATA COMPARISONS

"Hey, Jack," Erik said. "Why did the computer wear glasses?"

"Erik," Jack responded, "computers don't wear glasses."

"To fix its websight."

Jack shook his head. "Are you trying to get our reader to close the book?"

"They love it! Okay, did you know that two equal signs (==) means something special in Python?"

"That's right!" Jack answered. "Using two equal signs compares two pieces of data to see if they're equal (the same)."

"This is easiest to show by putting it to use," Jack explained. "Write this code in IDLE:"

```
>>> 4 == 4
```

"Press enter," Jack instructed. "We get True because four *is* equal to four. To get False, write this code in IDLE:"

```
>>> 4 == 5
```

"Press enter," Jack directed. "Four is *not* the same as 5."

"That's cool, Jack!" Erik announced. "Did you know we can compare variables in the same way? Write this in IDLE and press enter after each line:"

```
>>> Jack = 15
>>> Erik = 15
>>> Jack == Erik
```

"We get True!" Erik proclaimed. "Now write this in IDLE, pressing enter after each line:"

```
>>> Erik = 100
>>> 100 == Erik
```

"We get True again!" Erik yelled.

"So, Erik, did you know you can also make comparisons using words?" Jack asked.

"How does that work, Jack?"

"Well, I'll show you. The word AND can be used to see if two pieces of information are *both* True. Let's see this in action. Write this code in IDLE and press enter after each line:"

```
>>> Jack = 33
>>> Erik = 51
>>> Jack is 33 and Erik is 51
```

"We get True!" Jack announced. "In addition to using *and*, we actually used *is*. In Python, *is* means the same thing as the double equal sign (==) we used earlier. Meaning, *is* and == both check to see if the data on both sides is the same. Let's do another one. Write this code in IDLE:"

```
>>> 5 > 3 and 9 < 10
```

"It's True!" Jack proclaimed. "Five is larger than three and nine is smaller than 10! To get False, write this code in IDLE, pressing enter after each line:"

```
>>> Erik = 5
>>> Erik is 5 and 4 > 10
```

"Even though the variable name Erik was assigned the value 5 (meaning, it is True that Erik *is* 5), 4 is *not* bigger than 10," Jack explained, "that's why we get False. When we use *and*, *both* pieces of data must be True to return True."

"That's awesome, Jack!" Erik announced. "And we can use the word OR in Python. OR checks to see if one *or* both pieces of data are True. Let's see how this works by redoing the code we just wrote, using *or* instead of *and*. Write this code in IDLE, pressing enter after each line:"

```
>>> Erik = 5
>>> Erik is 5 or 4 > 10
```

"Now we get True!" Erik announced. "That's because at least one of the pieces of data is True. Remember, OR checks for one *or* both, but with AND *both* must be True. Let's show this by seeing what happens when both pieces of data are True. Write this code in IDLE:"

```
>>> 5 == 5 or 10 is 10
```

"Press enter," Erik instructed. "This is True because five is five and ten is ten. Now write this code in IDLE and press enter after each line:"

```
>>> Jack = "happy"
>>> Erik = "silly"
>>> Erik is "Silly" or Jack is "Happy"
```

"We got False!" Erik shouted. "Why? Because we capitalized Silly and Happy, which was incorrect because when we assigned the values to the variable, we wrote them in lowercase. The computer sees *Silly* and *silly*, as different things. Because both sides of *or* were False (not the same) we got False."

"I think I get it," Jack stated. "Another one we can use is *not*. It's easiest to explain by using it."

"Yeah," Erik agreed, "So go ahead and write this code in IDLE:"

```
>>> 5 is not 10 and Jack is not "Hilarious"
```

"And press enter," Erik instructed, "We get True! That's because 5 is not the same as 10, and Jack is not funny."

"Wow, Erik," Jack responded. "Okay, my turn. But first, did you know that you can use an ! (exclamation point) to mean *not*? Write this code in IDLE and press enter after each line:"

```
>>> Erik = 'dork'
>>> Erik != 'cool'
```

"The != says, 'Erik is not equal to cool,'" Jack explained.

"Moving on..." Erik said. "We can also combine the < and > operators with =. For example, >= means 'greater than *or* equal to' and <= means 'lesser than *or* equal to.' Write this code in IDLE and press enter after each line:"

```
>>> Jack = 20
>>> 20 >= Jack
```

"We get True!" Erik announced. "Because 20 is equal to Jack.

"Now, write this code in IDLE and press enter after each line:"

```
>>> Jack = 25
>>> Erik = 50
>>> 50 >= Jack
```

"We also get True!" Erik stated. "Because 50 is more than 25 (the value assigned to Jack)."

"Well, Erik," Jack said, "this has been one of our longest chapters, so I think we should end it with a challenge. To our friend, the reader, use the following operators in IDLE:"

- `==,`
- `is not,`
- `and,`
- `or,`
- `!=, and`
- `<=.`

As soon as you finished the challenge, Jack looked at Erik and said, "I can't believe the reader finished our challenge that fast!"

"Me either," Erik agreed, "I guess we will have to make the later ones harder!"

"In the next chapter, I think we can start doing some cooler things with our programs."

"I'm excited! Let's do this!"

CHAPTER NINE
IF

Jack and Erik were skydiving. As they flew through the air, Jack yelled over to Erik, "What do you call someone who has no body and no nose?"

"Ummm... A ghost with no sense of smell?" Erik guessed as the ground below them got closer and closer.

"Nobody knows," Jack answered.

Erik laughed so hard that he almost forgot to open his parachute! Jack didn't think the joke was that funny but he knew Erik would like it.

Thankfully, despite the dorky joke, they both landed safely on the ground right outside The Tech Academy.

"Well, Jack, my heart is racing!" Erik panted. "Let's get on with the book."

"Thank goodness this is all fictional because I would never skydive in real life," Jack admitted. "I'm too afraid of heights!"

Erik sat in front of a laptop and said, "An *if statement* is when you have the computer do something *if* another thing is True. For example, *if* I am hungry, *then* feed me waffles. Let's see how this works in Python. Write this code in IDLE and press enter two times:"

```
>>> if 5 > 3:
        print("Five is larger than three")
```

"Good job!" Erik acknowledged. "We just told the computer, 'If it is True that the number 5 is larger than the number 3, show the string (words) 'Five is larger than three'). Let's see what happens when we type something false. Write this code in IDLE and press enter two times:"

```
>>> if 10 > 20:
        print("Ten is larger than twenty")
```

"Nothing happens because it isn't True!" Erik announced.

"I see how that works, Erik," Jack said. "Write this code in IDLE and press enter after each line:"

```
>>> Jack = 34
>>> Erik = 51
>>> if Erik > Jack:
        print("Erik is older than Jack")
```

"That's pretty cool, Jack," Erik said. "You used variables within an if statement! What do we do if we want more than one choice?"

"We can use the *elif statement*," Jack replied, "which literally just gives another thing to check for."

"There's an elf in Python?!" Erik cried out.

"No, Erik. *Elif.* It's short for else/if. Something like, *'if* happy then laugh, *elif* sad then cry,' would say that you should laugh if you're happy or cry if you're sad."

"Ummm... How about we change *cry* to *dance*?! That always cheers me up!" Erik started dancing. "Everybody do The Gross!" Jack had to look away.

"Let's try this out," Jack said, as he tried to focus on something other than Erik's dance moves. "Write this code in IDLE, pressing enter after each line:"

```
>>> Happy = 50
>>> Sad = 100
>>> if Happy > Sad:
        print("Laugh")
```

```
elif Sad > Happy:
```

"Oh, no!" Jack cried. "We got an error!"

"That's because we didn't indent the code correctly," Erik explained.

"Indent?"

"You see the TAB key on your keyboard? That pushes the cursor (that small black line that flashes up and down on your screen that shows you where to type) over several spaces to the right. When you move text over like that, especially when pressing the TAB key, that's called indenting. If you noticed, Python was automatically indenting some of our code. Meaning, it was moving it to the right a little. The problem is that the elif statement shouldn't be indented. To fix this we need to press backspace (a key that moves text to the left and can delete things) on the line that has the elif statement to get rid of the indent. I'll show you. Write this code in IDLE and press enter after each line:"

```
>>> if Happy > Sad:
        print("Laugh!")
elif Sad > Happy:
        print("Shake your booty!")
```

"Now it should work!" Erik stated.

"Wow, that seems really silly," Jack stated.

"Well, it's all part of the rules on how to write Python," Erik explained. "Remember, we call these rules syntax. Now, Jack, what if we want three or more choices?"

"Thank you for asking. We can also use the *else statement*. What this does is say, 'Alright computer, when I wrote my if statement and elif statement, I told you what to do, but for anything *else* that happens, do this other thing. For example, *if* sleepy then go to bed, *if* dirty then take a shower, *else* then read this book. This basically says to sleep if you're tired, bathe if you're dirty, and to otherwise spend all your time reading this life-changing book! Write this code in IDLE, pressing enter after each line (and don't forget to move *elif* and *else* to the left with the backspace key!):"

```
>>> Color = "Blue"
>>> if Color is "Red":
        print("The color is red!")
elif Color is "White":
        print("The color is white!")
else:
        print("The color is blue!")
```

"What happened here is that the computer first checked to see if the color was Red (if statement), found it was False so moved to the next step, checked to see if the color was White (elif statement), found it was also False, then it said, 'If the Color is anything else besides Red or White, print 'The color is blue!' (else statement)," Jack explained.

"Whoa," Erik said, "that seems kind of complicated."

"I understand," Jack comforted. "It will get easier the more we play around with it. Let's try another one."

"Okay," Erik said. "Write this code in IDLE, pressing enter after each line:"

```
>>> if 1 + 1 == 3:
        print("one plus one is three!")
elif 2 + 2 == 4:
        print("two plus two is four!")
else:
        print("I can't math right now...")
```

"In this code, *elif* was True and so that was the one that printed!" Erik explained. "Now, it's time for a challenge! Perform the following actions in IDLE:"

- Write your own if statement,
- Write your own elif statement, and
- Write your own else statement.

Erik and Jack waited anxiously as the reader wrote if, elif and else statements that were just way better than the ones in this book. When the reader finished, they both did one-handed cartwheels through hoops of fire!

"Thank goodness we are just cartoons!" Erik yelled. "Otherwise that would have been very dangerous!"

Jack ended the chapter with a very short poem:
"This chapter has been interesting and fun,
But it is time we started another one."

CHAPTER TEN
LISTS

Erik walked into the office and found Jack fanning a wildebeest. "Jack?" Erik asked, "what are you doing?"

"He was hot!" Jack stated defensively.

"But-"

"I don't want to talk about it anymore."

"Okay..." Erik said with a pause. "Anyways, I really want to show the reader how to create a list in Python."

"What's a list?" Jack asked as the wildebeest trotted out of the room.

"It's just the normal meaning of *list* – like: red, blue, orange, etc."

"But isn't there a special Python meaning?"

"Not really. It's the same idea as the word *list* in English. Like a grocery list: Eggs, Cheese, Milk, presents for Jack, etc. That reminds me, I need to go shopping – I am all out of worm food!"

"Wait...don't worms just eat dirt?"

"Only the finest dirt for my worms!"

"And why do you own worms?"

Erik just whistled and spun around in his office chair.

"Back to the point," Jack started, "let's make a list. Write this code in IDLE and press enter after each line:"

```
>>> Family = ['Kelly', 'Mark', 'Maxine', 'Jack']
>>> print(Family)
```

"Jack!" Erik shrieked. "You just shared the real names of your family!"

"Yep, that's my mom, dad, sister and me!" Jack announced. "Okay, my turn for a random fact. When you start counting, you start at the number 1, right? Like 1, 2, 3, etc."

"Yes, I know how to count, Jack. Jeez..."

"Well, here's the random fact: computers start counting at 0! The first number is zero – not one! They go 0, 1, 2, 3, etc."

"I'm glad you said that because that connects with what I wanted to talk about. Alright, so first we need to understand the word 'index.'"

"Like the thing in a book that tells you what page different things are on?"

"Yeah, very similar to that. An index is the number of a value (one of the names) on a list. So, for example, here is the index for each value on the list you made:

VALUE:	VALUE:	VALUE:	VALUE:
Kelly	Mark	Maxine	Jack
INDEX:	INDEX:	INDEX:	INDEX:
0	1	2	3"

"Okay, smartie pants," Jack said, "can we write some more code now?"

"That's a great suggestion because I was going to explain that we look up (find) and print (show) values (names for the things in our list) using indexes. Let me show you. Write this code in IDLE and press enter after-"

"Hey Erik, I think we can stop telling them to press enter. They get it at this point."

"You're right! Write this code in IDLE:"

```
>>> Family = ['Emily', 'Violet', 'Magnus',
'Jack']
>>> print(Family[2])
```

"Cool, Erik!" Jack announced. "You displayed the name of my son (Magnus) by writing the index (number) of his name in the list. And you included my wife (Emily) and daughter (Violet) in this list!"

"Yeah!" Erik agreed. "Emily is 0, Violet is 1, Magnus is 2 and Jack is 3! And we can concatenate (connect) strings (sequence of characters) to values on our lists. Write this code in IDLE:"

```
>>> TechAcademy = ['Trisha', 'Brett', 'Briar',
'Danny', 'Patrick']
>>> print(TechAcademy[3] + " is a wonderful Tech
Academy employee!")
```

"I agree," Jack said, "Danny is wonderful! Hey, want to make the computer count?"

"Sure," Erik agreed. "How do we do that?"

"Get ready because the name of the command we use is very weird and has nothing to do with counting... It's called... the *counter!*"

"Ha! You almost got me there!"

"Now, remember way earlier in the book when we said there are actually two parts to IDLE? The shell (what we've been writing our code in this whole time) and the text editor. To write larger programs, it's much better to use the text editor. To do this, click File and then select New File:

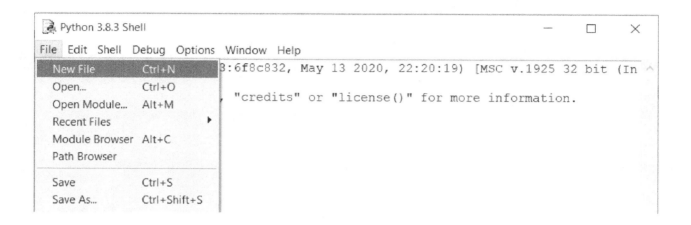

"You should see this:

"Now click File and then Save As.

"Now name your file Python.py and save the file on your Desktop. It is important to include the .py at the end of your file name, because that tells your computer, 'Hey! This is Python code!' If you leave it off, your code might not work right.

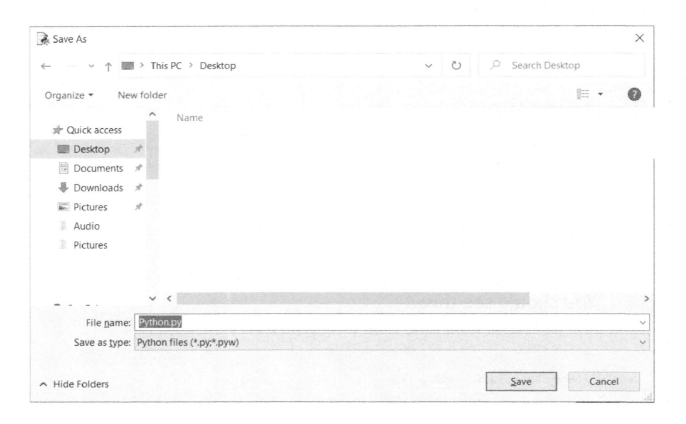

"Now, inside the text editor, write this code:"

```
counter = 0
print(counter)
counter = counter + 1
print(counter)
counter = counter + 2
print(counter)
counter = counter + 3
print(counter)
counter = counter - 6
print(counter)
```

"Now click save your code," Jack continued. "You can do this by clicking File and then selecting Save, or you can just press the *CTRL key* and the *S key* on your keyboard at the same time.

"You'll want to save the file on your desktop and name your file Python.py, like this:

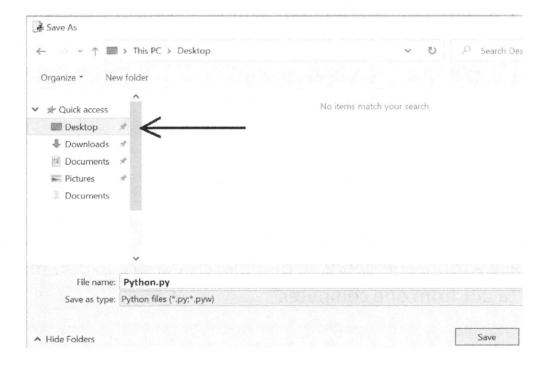

"*Always save your code before running it!*" Jack warned. Otherwise your program won't be up-to-date with any new data you added. Now to run the code you wrote, click on Run and then click Run Module. In normal English, a *module* is a part of something. In Python, a *module* is a bunch of code written by others that you can use in your programs. You can also create modules that you and other people can use. It's just code that makes up a program. So, when we say Run Module, we are saying execute (perform) my program."

"Whew!" Jack said. "You just made a program using the text editor! We can slow this down so the numbers come out one at a time. First, let's define the word *import* – *import* means to bring something in. Like if you import tea from England, tea is sent from England to America – it is brought into the U.S. It means the same in computers, to bring data in from elsewhere. So, what's the opposite of import?"

"Ummm... outport?" Erik guessed.

"Good guess, but I regret to inform you that you are absolutely and totally wrong. The opposite of *import* is *export*. *Export* means to send data out from one computer."

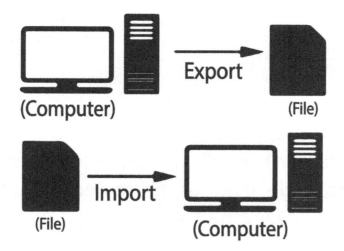

(Computer)   Export   (File)

(File)   Import   (Computer)

"Ah, I see where you're going with this..." Erik said. "You can import modules (groups of code written by others that you can use). For example, Python has a math module that you can use to do advanced math. To use these modules, you import them!"

"Well, Erik, you tied that up like a nice little bow!" Jack announced. "So, back to counting slower – write this code in the text editor:"

```
import time
counter = 0
print(counter)
time.sleep(.5)
counter = counter + 1
print(counter)
time.sleep(.5)
counter = counter + 2
print(counter)
time.sleep(.5)
counter = counter + 3
print(counter)
time.sleep(.5)
```

```
counter = counter - 6
print(counter)
time.sleep(.5)
```

"Save and execute your code. We counted with each number .5 seconds (half a second) apart!" Jack explained. "`time.sleep` is one of the functions (code that can be reused) included in the time module (code written by others that we can use), for causing delays in our programs."

"Interesting," Erik said. "It's that time again: challenge time! Okay, magical reader, write, save and run this code in the text editor:"

- Create a list and display (print) the whole thing,
- Print one value from the list, and
- Use the counter to count from 1 to 10 with a one second delay between each number.

While the reader completed the challenge, Erik and Jack rode a rocket into outer space to test something out. Once they were near the moon, they gazed back at Earth.

"Just as we thought," Erik said. "We can see the reader's awesomeness from space!"

"Houston, we *don't* have a problem," Jack announced.

"I think some people aren't going to get that..."

"Well, they just need to watch the movie *Apollo 13*."

"If we are recommending movies, I have a few that-"

"Erik!" Jack interrupted, "the book. The book, Erik."

"My apologies, Jackalope. Let's start the next chapter now."

CHAPTER ELEVEN
LOOPY

After their rocket landed back on Earth, Jack and Erik gave Elon Musk a high five and returned to The Tech Academy.

"I was thinking, Jack," Erik began, "one of the things that make computers different than people is that a computer can keep doing the same thing over and over forever but a person would go crazy if that happened to them."

"What do you mean?" Jack asked.

"Well, there's a thing in computers called a *loop*. A *loop* is a command to repeat something until something else happens. It loops around and around, over and over, like a circle."

"I'm getting dizzy, Erik."

"One of the most popular types of loops is the *while loop*. This means, 'While _____ is True, do _____.' For example, while fat, try to lose weight. It literally means, as long as this thing that I am telling you is true, go ahead and do this other thing that I told you to do. Here, let me show you. But as a warning first, after you run this next code, you will have to close IDLE to make this code stop."

"Erik, the reader hasn't used IDLE for a little bit. How do we open IDLE again?"

"Good question, Jack! Just type IDLE in the search bar on the bottom left of your screen and then click on it to open it. Now, type this code in IDLE:

```
>>> while 2 > 1:
        print("I am a crazy computer!")
```

"Shut it down!" Jack yelled.

"This is called an infinite loop!" Erik proclaimed. "It never ends! Again, close IDLE to stop it. If a person had to keep saying the same sentence forever, doing nothing else, they'd go crazy!"

"Ah, I see," Jack said, "computers don't care because they're not alive."

"It's alive!" Erik shouted as he began walking around like Frankestien's monster.

"No, it's *not* alive," Jack corrected. "Anyways, let's close (end) this loop. Write this code in IDLE:"

```
>>> while 2 > 1:
        print("I am a crazy computer!")
        break
```

"You broke it!" Erik yelled.

"No," Jack explained, "that was the break statement – it basically told the computer, 'Hey, let's take a break from this loop.'"

"My turn! My turn!" Erik squealed. "Write this code in IDLE:"

```
>>> import time
>>> number = 0
>>> while number < 10:
        number = number + 1
        print(number)
        time.sleep(.25)
```

Jack's mind was blown. "Erik, what the heck did we just do?" He asked.

"Well, first we imported *time*," Erik began. "Remember, we have to bring that module (group of code written by others) into our program in order to use the *time.sleep() function* (which slows things down). We will talk about functions in more detail later but they're basically chunks of code that you can use over and over again. Then we assigned the value o to our variable *number* – we said, 'The number is zero.' We then told the computer to cycle through (repeat) the loop as long as our number was smaller than 10. Then we told the computer to increase the value (amount) of our variable *number* by +1 – literally, 'Change it from zero to one.' After that we printed the new number. Then we did a quick .25 second (quarter of a second) pause and repeated the same thing over, increasing *number* by one each time, over and over until *number* reached ten!"

"That kinda makes sense. But I feel kinda confused. Maybe it will help if we do another one. Write this code in IDLE:"

```
>>> amount = 20
>>> while amount > 0:
        amount = amount - 1
        print(amount)
        time.sleep(.5)
```

"Wow!" Erik shouted in amazement. "That was like a rocketship countdown!"

"Yeah, so basically what we said was that the *amount* is twenty," Jack explained. "Then we said as long as the *amount* is more than zero, keep repeating this loop over and over. Once it reaches zero, stop. Then we subtracted one from the *amount* over and over, printing the new *amount* each time."

"Yep! And don't worry. The more code we write, the more sense this all makes!"

"I think it's time we talk about the other most popular type of loop. It's called a *for loop*. With the *while loop*, we didn't specify (clearly say) how many times to repeat the loop. Like we didn't say, repeat 10 times. With the *for loop*, we do specify how many times to repeat the loop. It means for _____ long, do _____. For example, for ten bites, eat – that would mean that we eat ten bites worth of food and then stop. One of the functions we can use with *for loops* is *range()*. The *range()* function can be used to display (show) a list of numbers within a certain range (limit; amount). So, now let's write a *for loop*. Write this code in IDLE:"

```
>>> import time
>>> for counter in range(1,11):
        print(counter)
        time.sleep(.5)
```

"Well done!" Jack announced. "We counted to ten!"

"That's the highest I've ever counted!" Erik shouted. "Jack, what did this code do?"

"Well, again," Jack began, "we imported time so we could have slight delays in between printing numbers using time.sleep(). Then we said, 'Alright, computer, for each number between 1 and 11, print the number once.' Remember that counter is used to count up in Python."

"That's cool!" Erik said. "We're going to write another *for loop* but it's time to learn another new word! To *iterate* means to say or do something again; to repeat something. *Iteration* is the act of repeating. In coding, *iterate* means to go through steps and repeat them a certain number of times."

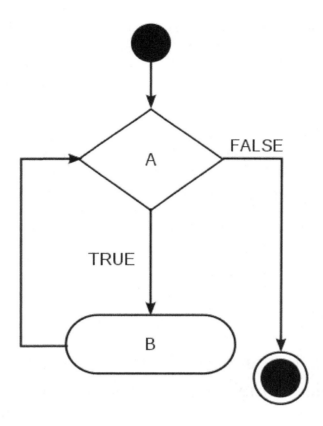

"This picture is a loop. *An iteration is one time through the loop.* To iterate through a loop means to go through it one time and then either repeat the loop or end off. Write this code in IDLE:"

```
>>> Colors = ["Red", "Blue", "Orange", "Yellow",
"Green"]
>>> for EachColor in Colors:
        print(EachColor + ' is a great color!')
```

"Okay..." Jack started. "Somehow that printed out *Colors*, but I have no idea how."

"Well," Erik began, "what we said was, for each color in our list, print the color. Since there are five colors in our list, we iterated through the list five times."

"Okay, so, basically 'loop' just means repeating things over and over. A *while loop* says, 'I don't quite know how many times I want to iterate (repeat or complete) this loop, but do it as long as _____ is happening (True). And a *for loop* means, 'repeat through this loop this many times.'"

"Yep! That's pretty much it!"

"I think this is the perfect time for a challenge. Okay, our breathtaking reader, complete the following in IDLE:

- `Write your own while loop, and`
- `Write your own for loop."`

Right when the reader completed the challenge, giant fireworks exploded over Jack's and Erik's heads. "Those came out of nowhere!" Erik shrieked.

"Yeah!" Jack agreed. "This reader is *explosive*!"

"Alright, Erik," Jack said, "let's write another chapter."

"We aren't ending the book here?" Erik questioned.

"No way! We have a lot more to cover."

"I'm in!"

CHAPTER TWELVE
DICTIONARIES

Jack walked into an empty office. *Where's Erik?* He thought. Jack looked around the office and then heard some heavy footsteps outside the window. He looked outside and saw Erik riding an ostrich!

"Yee-haw!" Erik shouted.

"Erik!" Jack yelled. "Put Sally away! We have work to do!"

Erik was so surprised that he jumped off Sally the ostrich and put his head in the sand.

The ostrich stared, shook her head and then trotted away. Erik walked into the office brushing sand out of his hair, while Jack swept the floor.

"Hey, Jack," Erik began, "why is this chapter called dictionaries? Is it because we want people to buy our *Technology Basics Dictionary: Tech and Computers Simplified?* Now available for purchase on Amazon!"

"You're selling again, Erik..." Jack warned.

"I can't help it!"

"That's okay. No, this chapter is not about big books used to define words. In Python, a *dictionary* is a special type of list. There are two things that make up a dictionary:

"1. **Key:** the name

"2. **Value:** the amount or type of something

"For example, this is a dictionary:

KEY	VALUE
Video game	Minecraft
Food	Cheeseburger
TV show	Avatar: The Last Airbender
Movie	Jurassic Park

"Each key in a dictionary can have multiple values. Like this:

KEY	VALUES
Pizza	Pepperoni, cheese, sauce
Sub sandwich	Turkey, cheddar cheese, mayonnaise, pickles
Salad	Lettuce, olives, tomatoes, cucumbers, ranch dressing."

"Thanks a lot!" Erik snorted. "Now I'm hungry!"

"You're always hungry!"

"Can't argue that. For me, this would be an infinite loop: `While Erik hungry, eat.`"

Jack laughed and said, "Let's create a dictionary in Python. Write this code in IDLE:"

```
>>> Things_Dictionary = {'Animal': 'cat', 'Toy':
'ninja turtle','Book': 'Animorphs'}
>>> print(Things_Dictionary)
```

"First of all, why did you have a _ in your code?" Erik asked.

"Well, _ is called an underscore," Jack explained. "A score is a mark – so an underscore is literally a mark that's under other text. Computer programmers sometimes use underscores instead of spaces to connect text. For example, Jack_Carl_Stanley instead of Jack Carl Stanley. It's just something we do."

"Okay. Second of all, what are Animorphs?" Erik inquired.

"Are you kidding me? It's an amazing book series by the author K.A. Applegate about a group of kids that can change (morph) into animals and they use these powers to fight evil aliens!"

"I wish I could turn into an ostrich…" Erik said as he gazed longingly out the window, thinking about Sally. After a few moments, Erik gathered his composure and said, "I want to add something to the dictionary! Write this code in IDLE:"

```
>>> Things_Dictionary['Best_Bird'] = 'Ostrich'
>>> print("The best bird is an: " +
Things_Dictionary['Best_Bird'])
```

"We just added something to the dictionary, pulled it out of the dictionary and displayed it!" Erik explained.

"Okay," Jack started, "write this code in IDLE:"

```
>>> del Things_Dictionary['Best_Bird']
>>> print(Things_Dictionary)
```

"Hey!" Erik shouted. "You deleted my ostrich!"

"I was just showing the reader how to delete things from the dictionary!" Jack said defensively. "In our code, del is short for delete."

"Okay, okay. Anyways, my *real* ostrich is in the barn eating worms."

So that's what the worms are for, Jack thought.

"Let's do a challenge," Erik stated. "Okay, reader! See if you can do this in IDLE:"

- Create a dictionary and print it,
- Add something to your dictionary,
- Delete something from your dictionary, and
- Display the dictionary again (after you've added and deleted something).

As Jack and Erik watched the reader create the best dictionary they'd ever seen, their mouths opened so wide that their jaws smashed onto their toes! "Ow!" they both shouted right when the reader finished.

"You're so good at this it hurts!" Jack proclaimed. "Mommy!" Erik cried.

Jack rubbed his feet and said, "Let's learn some more cool things you can do with Python."

"Onto the next chapter!" Erik announced.

CHAPTER THIRTEEN
FUNCTIONS

"Hey, Jack," Erik started, "how did the coder get out of prison?"

"Oh, no..." Jack complained.

"He used the escape key!"

Jack left the office and took a three-hour walk. He then came back, walked in and sat down.

"Welcome back, Jack!" Erik yelled as he clapped his hands together. "Hey, that rhymed!"

Jack cleared his throat and said, "Alright... So... Let's continue with the book. In normal English, a *function* is someone's job – it is an action they do. For example, it is a function of police to arrest bad guys. In coding, a *function* is a chunk of code that does a particular thing. The cool thing about functions is that you can reuse them. As an example, you could have a function that plays sound every time the user clicked their mouse."

"What's a user?" Erik asked.

"Oh, just someone who uses something. It usually means 'the person using the computer.'"

"Ah, yes, I am a frequent user of the waffle iron."

"Waffles... Slightly crunchy pancakes with little pockets of buttery-syrup joy."

"Back to the book! To make a function in Python we use the *def* command. *Def* is short for *define*, which means to say exactly what something is. Write this code in IDLE:"

```
>>> def Subtraction(Number1, Number2):
        subtract = Number1 - Number2
        return subtract

>>> print(Subtraction(20, 10))
>>> print(Subtraction(10, 5))
>>> print(Subtraction(500, 350))
```

"Wow!" Erik shouted. "To explain what our code did here, let's start with what the word *parameters* means."

"Paragraph?" Jack asked.

"No, parameters."

"Pennsylvania?"

"No, J- Oh, I see what you're doing here. Good one! In normal English, *parameters* refers to the limit of something – literally, how much space something takes up or, figuratively, what is included within a particular subject."

Jack yawned.

"For example," Erik continued, "talking about waffles is outside the parameters of this book – meaning, it isn't included in the subject; it's off topic. In coding, *parameters* is the data your program needs in order to do things. It's the information used by your program."

"Okay... So, what are the parameters in the last program we wrote?" Jack asked.

Erik answered, "Well, first of all, this code is our function:

```
>>> def Subtraction(Number1, Number2):
        subtract = Number1 - Number2
        return subtract
```

"Alright," Jack acknowledged.

"**Number1** and **Number2** are the parameters," Erik explained.

"So, the data in the parentheses in our function is called the *parameters*?"

"Exactly! We named our function *Subtraction*. See, the name of a function comes after *def*."

"Ah, I see."

"What this function does is automatically subtract any two numbers that we choose! In our code, we named our variable *subtract* and assigned it the value of *Number1 - Number2* – we told the computer, 'Hey, so the word subtract is the same as whatever Number1 minus Number2 is.'"

"Yeah, I remember the whole variable thing."

"Great! Now, do you see the word *return* in our code?"

"Uh-huh."

"Functions are also called *subprograms*. *Sub-* means *under* or *lower* than. A *subprogram* is a smaller program inside your program. When you run a subprogram, the program passes all control over to the subprogram and when the subprogram is done running, we *return* to the main program."

"My goodness! This is a lot of words to learn!"

"Take a look at this picture:"

PROGRAM

Code executes...

Code executes...

SUBPROGRAM

Code executes...

"Oh, I get it," Jack said. "So, our function is a subprogram – a program within our program – and *return* tells the computer to go back to our main program."

"Perfecto!" Erik announced. "*Return* also does something else, it-"

"Aw man..."

"I understand it can seem like a lot to take in but this is the last thing I'm going to say before we write more code. *Return* also returns (sends data back to us) the result of our function. But just because the data was returned, doesn't mean it displays – we have to use the print statement to show the data that was returned. So, now the code we wrote should make more sense – here it is again for you to review:"

```
>>> def Subtraction(Number1, Number2):
        subtract = Number1 - Number2
        return subtract

>>> print(Subtraction(20, 10))
>>> print(Subtraction(10, 5))
>>> print(Subtraction(500, 350))
```

"I guess this all kinda makes sense..." Jack said.

"Don't worry," Erik said, "you'll get more used to it as we make more functions. Write this code in IDLE:"

```
>>> def Multiplication(FirstNumber,
SecondNumber, ThirdNumber):
        multiply = FirstNumber * SecondNumber *
ThirdNumber
        return multiply

>>> print(Multiplication(2, 4, 6))
```

"You should get 48!" Erik proclaimed. "We created a function here named Multiplication and we gave it three parameters: FirstNumber, SecondNumber and ThirdNumber. We told it that our variable *multiply* was the same amount as the FirstNumber multiplied by the SecondNumber and the ThirdNumber. Then we said to multiply those numbers, return the amount, then return to the program and print the results of multiplying 2 by 4 by 6."

"Alright," Jack acknowledged, "we will create more functions later in this book. But for now I want to show some other cool things that Python can do. Let's break up a date into parts using the date.split(/) command. Write this code in IDLE:"

```
>>> date = "3/13/2022"
>>> split_the_date = date.split('/')
>>> print(split_the_date)
>>> print(split_the_date[0])
>>> print(split_the_date[1])
>>> print(split_the_date[2])
```

"That's pretty cool!" Erik stated. "Hey, did you notice that we used the indexes (0, 1, 2) to display specific parts of the dates?"

"Yeah, that's right," Jack answered. "Computers start counting at 0 and each item on a list or in a sequence is assigned a number: 0, 1, 2, etc."

"Now, let's make our last program a little more useful. Write this code in IDLE:"

```
>>> date = "12/25/2025"
>>> full_date = date.split('/')
>>> print('The month is: ' + full_date[0] +
' The day is: ' + full_date[1] + ' The year is:
' + full_date[2])
```

"Cool!" Jack said. "Did you know that we can also change lowercase text to uppercase and vice versa? We do this using the swapcase() function. Swap means to switch two things. Write this code in IDLE:"

```
>>> Name = "Erik"
>>> Name.swapcase()
```

"That's interesting!" eRIK said. "Okay, I think we should now have our dear reader write a lot of code all at once! This will use a lot of what we've learned so far. Create a new file in the text editor and-"

"Wait!" Jack interrupted. "How do we open the text editor again?"

"Oh, yes! Inside IDLE, you click File and then New File. So, again, open a new file in the text editor and write this code:

```python
MathFun = "Let's do some math!"
print(MathFun)
Number1 = 10
print("Number1 = 10")
print("Number1 plus 5 equals:")
print(Number1 + 5)
Number2 = 5
print("Number2 = 5")
print("Number2 minus Number1 equals:")
print(Number2 - Number1)
print("Number1 times Number2 equals:")
print(Number1 * Number2)
print("Number1 divided by Number2 equals:")
print(Number1 / Number2)
print("Is Number1 larger than Number2?:")
print(Number1 > Number2)
print("Is Number1 less than Number2?:")
print(Number1 < Number2)
print("Are Number1 and Number2 equal?:")
print(Number1 == Number2)
if Number1 > Number2:
    print("Number1 (being 10) is larger than Number2 (which is 5)")
list_names = ['Billy', 'Sally', 'Johnny', 'Raphael']
print("Here's the list we created: ")
print(list_names)
print("Here's the third name from the list we wrote in ALL CAPS: " +
    list_names[2].upper())
date = "August/13th/1985"
print("Here's the date we created: " + date)
split_date = date.split('/')
print("Here's the date we entered split apart: ")
print(split_date)
another_name = 'EmiLy'
print("We chose the name: " + another_name)
print("Here's " + another_name + " written with the cases swapped: " +
    another_name.swapcase())
```

"Now, save and run your code," Erik directed.

"Whoa!" Jack yelled. "That's a lot of code!"

"Yep," Erik agreed. "But it's mostly things we've done already."

"Now, IT'S TIME!" Erik yelled dramatically. Erik was suddenly on a stage. In the audience was only one person, his mom. Erik was wearing a fake purple velvet robe and holding a plastic skeleton head. He then said (dramatically), "You can doubt that the stars are fire... You can doubt that the sun moves... You can doubt the truth and think it's a lie... But never doubt that I love!"

Erik's mom clapped.

"Ummmm..." Jack began. "I don't quite know what to say. I think this is a good time for a challenge. Okay, our popular reader, do the following in IDLE:"

● Print something,

- Assign a variable,
- Perform a math function, and
- Use an if statement.

Erik took off his (fake) velvet robe and stood in his normal clothes. He was still holding the plastic head. As Erik watched the reader perform the challenge, he squeezed the skull in excitement. Suddenly, just as the reader finished the challenge, the skeleton head exploded and pieces of plastic chunks flew all over the room.

Jack ducked and then applauded in amazement at how well the reader did at the challenge.

"Let's take a look at some other cool things we can do with Python!" Erik announced.

"Sounds good!" Jack agreed. "Onto the next chapter!"

CHAPTER FOURTEEN
PYTHON FUNCTIONS

The bull was charging. Jack held a red cape. The bull came closer with only one thing on it's mind, *destroy the color red*. The bull's horns brushed against the cape as Jack performed a triple backflip, successfully escaping the spiky horns. Erik clapped as he chewed on buttery popcorn with Milk Duds mixed in.

"Bravo!" Erik cheered.

Jack put the cape down and gave the bull a high five.

"Same time next week?" The bull asked.

"You know that's right!" Jack confirmed.

The bull trotted off.

"I love that we can make animals talk in our book!" Erik said.

"Why didn't we make the ostrich talk?" Jack asked.

"She was talking. You just couldn't hear her because her head was in the sand."

"Erik, let's get the story straight, *your* head was in the sand."

Erik quickly changed the subject. "What's the difference between the number 5 and 5.5?"

"One has a dot and one doesn't."

"That's right! One is a whole number and one is a decimal number. A decimal number is one that contains a fraction – meaning a part of something. For example, using a decimal number, the amount nine-and-a-half, would be written as 9.5. In coding, a decimal number is called a *floating pointing* number."

"Wait… So, it's a number with a bunch of dots floating in the air?"

"Well, you're right that the *point* in *floating point* number refers to the decimal point (the dot)," Erik answered. "The *float* part just means that the dot can float around (move) depending on the number. For example, 3.25 versus 34.755 – the decimal point is in different places in these two numbers."

"So, we call decimal point numbers *floating point* numbers when coding?" Jack asked.

"Yeah, or just *float* for short. So, remember how we just talked about functions? As a reminder, a *function* is a chunk of code that does something and can be reused whenever you want. There are many functions already built into Python. What this means is that Python automatically includes these functions in it. The *float()*

© Prosper Consulting Inc., The Tech Academy

function returns a floating point number from an integer (whole number) or string (sequence of characters). Write this code in IDLE:"

```
>>> Number = float(699)
>>> print(Number)
```

"You have turned an integer (whole number) into a floating point (decimal) number!" Erik explained. "Now let's do the opposite. Let's change a float into an integer. To do this we use the *integer()* function. Write this code in IDLE:"

```
>>> Amount = 219.67
>>> print(Amount)
>>> Whole_Number_Amount = int(Amount)
>>> print(Whole_Number_Amount)
```

"We got rid of the fraction!" Erik announced. "No more float (decimal)! Or we can round a float number to the nearest whole number (integer) by using the round function. Write this code in IDLE:

```
>>> Floating_Point_Number = 29.76521
>>> print(round(Floating_Point_Number))
```

"Whoa!" Jack yelled. "It rounded up to 30! Another function is the *len()* function. This gets the length (number of characters) of a variable (such as a string or integer). Write this code in IDLE:"

```
>>> How_many_characters = len("I am learning a lot from this Python book!")
```

```
>>> print(How_many_characters)
```

"See how it counted the total characters and spaces?" Jack asked. "Let's try it with numbers. Write this code in IDLE:"

```
>>> How_many_numbers = len("1234567891011121314
151617181920")
>>> print(How_many_numbers)
```

"Boom!" Erik yelled.

"We can also delete variables," Jack explained. "Write this code in IDLE:"

```
>>> Number = 15
>>> print(Number)
>>> del Number
>>> print(Number)
```

"As you can see," Jack began, "you get an error message after you delete because *Number* is no longer stored! Can you guess what *del* is short for?"

"Delaware?" Erik guessed.

"Wow... It's short for *delete!*"

"Or we can try this:"

```
>>> del Erik
```

"It didn't work!" Jack complained. "You're still here!"

"Hahaha," Erik laughed sarcastically. "Did you know another common thing that programmers do is assign number values to variables that are named as letters?"

Jack fell asleep.

"What I mean is it's common to see things like X = 5 or A = 10, or whatever. This is because you sometimes see this in math. But it's more likely that computer programmers do this because sometimes they're kinda lazy." Jack woke up.

Erik said, "Write this code in IDLE:"

```
>>> A = 10
>>> B = 20
>>> X = 30
>>> print(a + b + x)
```

"Oops!" Erik shrieked. "Oh yeah, I remember now. It's case sensitive. Meaning, we have to use the same upper or lowercase that we used when we created the variables in the beginning. So, write *this* code in IDLE:"

```
>>> A = 10
>>> B = 20
>>> X = 30
>>> print(A + B + X)
```

"We get 60!" announced Erik.

"Interesting, so people sometimes name variables as letters – okay, fine," Jack said.

"Yep! Now let's put together all we've learned so far. Write this code in the text editor:"

```python
import time
X = 10
print("X (10) is not equal to 15:")
time.sleep(.5)
print(X != 15)
print("X is greater than or equal to 15:")
time.sleep(.5)
print(X >= 15)
if X <= 15:
    print("X is not equal to or greater than 15.")
    time.sleep(.5)
number = 25
if number == 15:
    print("25 is not equal to 15.")
else:
    print("The number is 25.")
    time.sleep(.25)

counter = 25
print(counter)
time.sleep(.25)
counter = counter +5
print(counter)
time.sleep(.25)
counter = counter - 28
print(counter)
time.sleep(.25)
```

```python
counter = counter * 2
print(counter)
time.sleep(.25)
counter = counter / 3
print(counter)
time.sleep(.25)
for counter in range(2,6):
    print(counter)
    time.sleep(.25)
for counter in range(10,4,-1):
    print(counter)
    time.sleep(.25)
while counter < 22:
    print(counter + 2)
    counter = counter + 4
    time.sleep(.25)

list = ["a", "b", "c", "d", "e", "f", "g", "etc."]
print(list)
time.sleep(.25)
dictionary = {'Apple' : 'Fruit', 'Bush' : 'Plant',
              'Carrot' : 'Vegetable'}
print(dictionary)
time.sleep(.25)
print('Now we will add "dog" to the dictionary.')
time.sleep(.25)
dictionary['Dog'] = 'Animal'
print(dictionary)
time.sleep(.25)
del dictionary['Apple']
print('Now, we have deleted "Apple" from the dictionary:')
print(dictionary)
```

"Save and execute your code," Erik instructed.

"Yee-haw!" Jack yelled. "That was another long one!"

"Yes siree!" Erik agreed.

Suddenly, Jack and Erik both had on cowboy hats and boots.

"Are you thinking what I'm thinking?" Jack asked.

"Why yes, I am," Erik agreed. "It's time for a challenge! Okay, Sheriff (that's you, the reader), why don't you go on and write a program in IDLE or the text editor that uses all of the following (it's totally okay to look back earlier in the book for reminders)?:"

- Float function,
- Integer function,
- Round function,
- Length function,
- Delete,
- If statement, elif statement and else statement,
- For loop,
- While loop, and
- Dictionary.

Jack and Erik danced a jig as the reader did the challenge. Then right when the reader finished, they jumped in the air and clicked their heels!

"Oh, boy!" Jack announced. "We are learning a lot in this book!"

"Well," Erik began, "let's get on with the next chapter because there's a lot more cool things you can do with Python!"

CHAPTER FIFTEEN
INPUT

"Stampede!" Jack shouted!

"Eeeek!" Erik screamed.

Jack and Erik ran as a herd of giant turtles stomped towards them.

"I thought turtles were supposed to be slow!" Jack yelled.

They kept running but the stampede got closer and closer. Suddenly, Sally the ostrich ran past the herd, and Jack and Erik jumped on her back. Then she flapped her tiny wings and they all slowly floated into the air.

"But, wait... Ostriches can't fly!" Jack stated.

"Believe, Jack," Erik begged, "*believe!*"

The giant turtles passed under them and Sally glided safely to The Tech Academy.

"Well, that was an interesting way to start this day," Erik said.

"Just another day at The Tech Academy," Jack replied.

"So, you know how in games and websites, you sometimes type in data, like your name and email address? How do you do that in Python?" Erik asked.

"Great question! Remember, that word we mentioned earlier, *input?* It means to put data into the computer. The *input()* function allows the user to enter information. Write this code in the text editor:"

```
color = input('Please enter your favorite color: ')
print("Your favorite color is " + color + "!")
```

"Save and execute your code," Jack instructed.

"Wow!" Erik shouted. "Our programs are getting more useful. Write this code in the text editor and then save and execute your code:

```
print('We are going to find out whether or not you like candy.')
Candy = input('Do you like candy?:')
if Candy == 'Yes':
    print('You like candy!')
elif Candy == 'No':
    print('You do not like candy.')
else:
    print('Please enter Yes or No exactly.')
```

"Cool!" Jack said. "But I have to type *Yes* or *No* with perfect capitalization and everything. What if I want to type *yes* (lowercase) or just *y?*"

"Oh," Erik began, "we would change our code. Write this code in the text editor and save and execute the code:"

```
print('We are going to find out whether or not you like candy.')
Candy = input('Do you like candy?: ')
if(Candy == 'Yes' or Candy == 'Y' or Candy == 'yes' or Candy == 'y'):
    print('You like candy!')
elif(Candy == 'No' or Candy == 'N' or Candy == 'no' or Candy == 'n'):
    print('You do not like candy.')
else:
    print('Please answer with one of the following: Yes, Y, yes, y, No, N, no, or n.')
```

"Awesome!" Jack said. "Now, create new file in the text editor and write this code:"

```python
print('Let us find out if you love to eat pizza!')
Cheese = input('Do you love pizza?: ')
if(Cheese == 'Yes' or Cheese == 'Y' or Cheese == 'yes' or Cheese == 'y'):
    print('You love pizza!')
elif(Cheese == 'No' or Cheese == 'N' or Cheese == 'no' or Cheese == 'n'):
    print('You do not love pizza!')
else:
    print('Please answer with one of the following: Yes, Y, yes, y, No, N, no, or n.')
```

"Now," Jack continued, "save and run your code."

"That's great!" Erik yelled. "Now, let's make a program that will store information about people and then grab data (like height, weight, birth year, etc.) by typing in their name. The first step will be to create a dictionary so we can easily handle the information. Then we will want to take information from the dictionary to show it to the user. Delete your code in the text editor (or create and save a new, separate file). Then write this code in the text editor:"

```python
people_dictionary={'Brett':['Male', 'Weight 175'],
            'Nancy':['Female', 'Weight 125'],
            'Patrick':['Male', 'Weight 195'],
            'Briar':['Female', 'Weight 115'],
            'Adam':['Male', 'Weight 215']}
print(people_dictionary)
Name = input('Please pick a name from the dictionary and type it here: ')
print('You typed in the name ' + Name + ' and here is their data: ')
Persons_Data = people_dictionary[Name]
print(Persons_Data)
```

"Save and run your code," Erik instructed. "If you receive an error, it means you didn't type a name exactly right. Otherwise, it will run!"

"This is all really cool!" Jack said. "How do we make a program that works even if someone enters the wrong name in?"

"Well," Erik started, "we can use the built-in Python functions *try* and *except*. These mean basically what they sound like. *Try* tries to find something in the dictionary. If *try* finds the thing in the dictionary, the program does what it's supposed to. If *try* doesn't find it, *except* takes over. *Except* gives another action for the program to do when something isn't found in the dictionary. Let's 'try' this out. Delete your code in the text editor (or create and save a new, separate file). Then write this code in the text editor:"

```python
people_dictionary = {'Brett':['Male', 'Weight 175'],
                     'Nancy' : ['Female', 'Weight 125'],
                     'Patrick' : ['Male', 'Weight 195'],
                     'Briar' : ['Female', 'Weight 115'],
                     'Adam' : ['Male', 'Weight 215']}
print(people_dictionary)
Name = input('Please pick a name from the dictionary and type it here: ')
print('You typed in the name ' + Name +
      ' and here is their data:')
try:
    Persons_Data = people_dictionary[Name]
    print(Persons_Data)
except:
    print("I'm sorry! That name was not found.")
```

"Save and run your program," Erik directed.

"As you may have noticed," Erik continued, "if you don't enter a name exactly as it's written in the dictionary, the program will think the name isn't there. Run your program again and type *brett* or *PATRICK* (instead of Brett or Patrick). It doesn't work!"

"I know what to do!" Jack announced. "To fix this, we can change the text the user types by using the *lower() method*. A method is code in Python that does something – it performs an action. The reason we want to force the text to lowercase (using the *lower() method*) is so that the text matches the text in our dictionary. Go ahead and take a look at the dictionary in your code – all the names are lowercase! Then, to display the names correctly (with the first letter capitalized) we can use the *capitalize() method*. Let's see this in action. Delete your code in the text editor (or create and save a new, separate file). Then write this code in the text editor:"

```python
print('Welcome to my program!')
people_dictionary = {'brett':['Male', 'Weight 175'],
                     'nancy' : ['Female', 'Weight 125'],
                     'patrick' : ['Male', 'Weight 195'],
                     'briar' : ['Female', 'Weight 115'],
                     'adam' : ['Male', 'Weight 215']}
Name = input('Please type in a name: ').lower()
try:
    Persons_Data = people_dictionary[Name]
    print('Here is their name: ' + Name.capitalize())
    print('Are they male or female? ' + Persons_Data[0])
    print('They weigh this much: ' + Persons_Data[1])
except:
    print('That name (as written) was not found in the dictionary.')
```

"Save and run your code," Jack instructed. "Try entering one of the names in ALL CAPS – it works!

"Wow, cool!" Erik said excitedly. "Now, how do we allow people to search for more names or search again when they don't type the name correctly? First, we need to define a start point to our program (which will allow us to have people go to the beginning of the program again). To do so, add this to the beginning of our code:"

```
def start():
```

"We are telling the computer, 'This is the beginning of our program!'" Erik explained. "If each line of your code following *def start()* doesn't automatically indent (go over the the right a few spaces), you will need to add one indentation per line of code (meaning, you'll have to press the TAB key for each line of code following *def start()*). Now, add this at the end of your code:"

```
start()
```

"Putting this at the end of our program makes it so that when our program hits that step, it starts over!" Erik said. "Now let's add another step to the program that lets the user search for another name. At the near end of your code, right above/before start(), write this code:"

```
def more():
    More = input('Would you like to search for another name?')
    if More == 'No':
        quit()
    if More == 'Yes':
        start()
    else:
        print("Please enter Yes or No.")
        more()
```

"As you probably guessed, *quit()* ends the program," Jack explained. "And *more()* is the name of our function (chunk of code that can be reused). What we are saying here is that after our program runs through once, we are gonna check if the person wants to do it again (do they want to do *more*?). If not, we shut down the program with *quit()*. If yes, we go back to the start of the program. If they don't enter 'Yes' or 'No,' we say, 'Please enter Yes or No,' then we go back to the beginning of the more() function."

"That's right, Jack," Erik said, "Now, we need to connect the *start()* section of our code to the *more()* section of our code, and we need to add *more()* to the end of the *try()* function, like this:"

```
try:
    Persons_Data = people_dictionary[Name]
    print('Here is their name: ' + Name.capitalize())
    print('Are they male or female? ' + Persons_Data[0])
    print('They weigh this much: ' + Persons_Data[1])
    more()
```

"And," Erik continued, "we need to add the *more()* function at the end of the *except* function:"

```
except:
    print('That name (as written) was not found in the dictionary.')
    more()
```

"Stop!" Jack yelled. "It's too much! I am so confused!"

"Don't worry," Erik comforted, "here is what your final code should look like this:"

```
def start():
    print('Welcome to my program!')
    people_dictionary = {'brett':['Male', 'Weight 175'],
                         'nancy' : ['Female', 'Weight 125'],
                         'patrick' : ['Male', 'Weight 195'],
                         'briar' : ['Female', 'Weight 115'],
                         'adam' : ['Male', 'Weight 215']}
    Name = input('Please type in a name: ').lower()
    try:
        Persons_Data = people_dictionary[Name]
        print('Here is their name: ' + Name.capitalize())
        print('Are they male or female? ' + Persons_Data[0])
        print('They weigh this much: ' + Persons_Data[1])
        more()
    except:
        print('That name (as written) was not found in the dictionary.')
        more()
def more():
    More = input('Would you like to search for another name? ')
    if More == 'No':
        quit()
    if More == 'Yes':
        start()
    else:
        print("Please enter Yes or No.")
        more()
start()
```

"Save and run the program," Erik directed. "Now you have a fully operational program!"

"Awesome!" Jack announced. "Another cool thing we can do with Python is alphabetize lists. We can do this using the sort() method. We are going to leave the text editor and use the IDLE shell again. So, open up IDLE and write this code:"

```
>>> Animals = ['Frog', 'Dog', 'Bat', 'Alligator', 'Cat', 'Elephant']
>>> print(Animals)
>>> Animals.sort()
>>> print(Animals)
```

"Whoa!" Erik cut in. "What about numbers?"

"Yep!" Jack answered. "It can sort numbers too – lowest to highest. Write this code in IDLE:"

```
>>> Amounts = [8, 2, 5, 3, 9, 1, 19, 4, 7, 6]
>>> print(Amounts)
>>> Amounts.sort()
>>> print(Amounts)
```

"Wow!" Erik shouted. "That was awesome! Wow, we really have learned a lot so far."

"The best part of this is that we will start combining all of these things soon to make some really cool programs!" Jack said.

"Oh, I see," Erik said. "This whole time we've been teaching one thing at a time so that we can bring it all together later!"

"Exactly!" Jack acknowledged.

"Okay, I have an idea," Erik began. "Let's make a program that figures out how long you've been alive! To do this, we will need to use two new Python functions *int()* and *str()*. *int()* is a function that turns input (what the user types) to a number – *int* is short for *integer* (whole number). *str()* is a function that turns input into a string (text). To make this program, we will want to use the text editor again. Right click on the Python.py file and select *Edit with IDLE*:

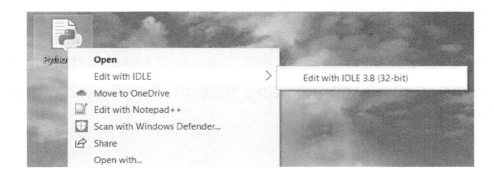

"If you can't find your code file, just open up a new file in the text editor," Jack directed.

"Now," Erik continued, "delete all the code in the file and write the following (as a note, if you want, you can create a New File instead and save it):"

```
Name = input('Name: ')
print("Hello " + Name +
     "! We are going to find out how long you've been alive!")
Age = int(input('How old are you? '))
print("You are " + str(Age) + " years old.")
Months = Age * 12
Days = Age * 365
print(Name + " has been alive for about: " + str(Months) +
     " months and " + str(Days) + " days!")
```

"Now before we run this code," Erik started, "let's talk about what some of the above code means. The *Age * 12* is saying that we are going to multiply the user's age by 12 months so we can figure out how many months they've been alive. The *Age * 365* says multiplies their age by 365 to figure out how many days the user has been alive. Now, save and run your program!"

"That's cool!" Jack said. "Let's take it a step further and figure out about how many minutes and seconds the user has been alive! Change your code to this:"

```
Name = input('Name: ')
print("Hello " + Name +
     "! We are going to find out how long you've been alive!")
Age = int(input('How old are you? '))
print("You are " + str(Age) + " years old.")
Months = Age * 12
Days = Age * 365
Minutes = Age * 525948
Seconds = Age * 31556926
print(Name + " has been alive for about: " + str(Months) +
     " months and " + str(Days) + " days " + str(Minutes) +
     " minutes and " + str(Seconds) + " seconds!")
```

"As a note, there are 525,948 minutes in a year and 31,556,926 seconds in a year!" Jack explained. "Save and run your code."

"Okay, we've covered a lot in this book," Erik said. "I want to make sure the reader is following along okay."

"Of course they are! How could you doubt our marvelous reader?!"

"I don't doubt them at all! But practice makes perfect! Okay, our superhero reader, we have another challenge for you. Do the following in IDLE:"

1. Assign an integer to a variable.

HINT:

```
>>> X = 10
```

2. Assign a string to a variable.

HINT:

```
>>> StarWars = "May the force be with you."
```

3. Assign a float to a variable.

HINT:

```
>>> DecimalNumber = 3.14
```

4. Use the print() function to print out the variable you assigned.

HINT:

```
>>> Name = "Jerick"
>>> print(Name)
```

5. Use each of these math operators:

a. +

HINT:

```
>>> 10 + 5
```

b. *

HINT:

```
>>> 5 * 10
```

c. /

HINT:

```
>>> 36 / 6
```

6. Use each of these comparison operators:

a. and

HINT:

```
>>> 4 > 3 and 25 < 20
```

b. or

HINT:

```
>>> 30 > 20 or 10 < 5
```

c. not

HINT:

```
>>> X = 25
>>> X is not 12
```

7. Use each conditional statement:

a. if

HINT:

```
>>> if 100 > 50:
        print('100 is more than 50!')
```

b. elif

HINT:

```
>>> if 100 > 250:
        print('100 is more than 250!')
elif 100 < 250:
        print('100 is less than 250!')
```

c. else

HINT:

```
>>> if 500 > 1000:
        print('500 is more than 1000!')
elif 1000 > 2000:
        print('1000 is more than 2000!')
else:
        print('None of these things are true!')
```

8. Use a *while* loop.

HINT:

```
>>> Number = 1
>>> while Number < 5:
        print(Number)
        Number += 1
```

9. Use a *for* loop.

HINT:

```
>>> Fruits = ['Oranges', 'Bananas', 'Apples']
>>> for Each_One in Fruits:
        print(Each_One)
```

10. Define a function that returns a string variable.

HINT:

```
>>> def My_function():
        print("This is my function")
>>> My_function()
```

11. Create a list of numbers and sort it.

HINT:

```
>>> Numbers = [80, 20, 50, 30, 90, 10, 100, 40,
70, 60]
>>> Numbers.sort()
>>> print(Numbers)
```

12. Create a list of strings and alphabetize it.

HINT:

```
>>> Colors = ['Red', 'Yellow', 'Blue', 'Green',
'Black', 'Gray', 'White']
>>> Colors.sort()
```

```
>>> print(Colors)
```

As the reader nailed the challenge, Erik climbed into a huge cannon. Jack lit the fuse and counted down from 10. But the reader finished the challenge with 3 seconds left and the cannon exploded early! Erik flew across the sky and pulled out a skateboard. He then rode his skateboard down a rainbow and high-fived the reader!

"Cowabunga!" Jack yelled. "This reader is a coding master! So, Erik, this is all fine and dandy but what about making games and stuff with Python."

Erik set his skateboard down. Took off his kneepads and elbow pads, and stored it all in the closet with his helmet. Then he said, "Well, Jack, modern games have thousands and thousands of lines of code – some even have millions."

"You're right. And there are hundreds to thousands of people that work on some of these games…"

"But that doesn't mean we can't make very basic games in Python."

"That's exactly what we are going to do in the next chapter!"

CHAPTER SIXTEEN
ROCK, PAPER, SCISSORS

Jack and Erik played rock paper scissors. Jack played scissors, Eirk played paper. They played again – Erik played paper, Jack played scissors. Then they went another time, Jack played scissors and Erik played paper.

"Erik," Jack said, "I don't think you're understanding this. You *always* pick paper!"

"I'll get you someday," Erik promised. "Some day, you'll pick rock..."

Jack shook his head and marked the score on the chalkboard.

"I know!" Jack announced. "Let's make a rock, paper, scissors game in Python! Step one, create a new file in the text editor and save it as Rock_Paper_Scissors_Game.py on your desktop. Within this new file, write the following code:"

```python
def start():
    print('This is my Rock Paper Scissors Game!')
    Player_One = 'Jack'
    Player_Two = 'Erik'

    def choices(Player_One_Choice, Player_Two_Choice):
        if Player_One_Choice == 'rock' and Player_Two_Choice == 'paper':
            return('Paper covers Rock! ' + Player_Two + ' wins!')
        elif Player_One_Choice == 'paper' and Player_Two_Choice == 'rock':
            return('Paper covers Rock! ' + Player_One + ' wins!')
        elif Player_One_Choice == 'scissors' and Player_Two_Choice == 'paper':
            return('Scissors cuts paper! ' + Player_One + ' wins!')
        elif Player_One_Choice == 'rock' and Player_Two_Choice == 'scissors':
            return('Rock smashes Scissors! ' + Player_One + ' wins!')
        elif Player_One_Choice == 'paper' and Player_Two_Choice == 'scissors':
            return('Scissors cuts paper ' + Player_Two + ' wins!')
        elif Player_One_Choice == 'scissors' and Player_Two_Choice == 'rock':
            return('Rock smashes Scissors! ' + Player_Two + ' wins!')
        elif Player_One_Choice ==  Player_Two_Choice:
            return('Jack and Erik tied')
        else:
            return('Please type Rock, Paper or Scissors!')

    Player_One_Choose = input('Does ' + Player_One + ' choose Rock, Paper or Scissors? ').lower()
    Player_Two_Choose = input('Does ' + Player_Two + ' choose Rock, Paper or Scissors? ').lower()

    print(choices(Player_One_Choose, Player_Two_Choose))

    def Play_Again():
        Again = input('Would you like to play the game again? ').lower()
        if Again == 'No'.lower():
            quit()
        if Again == 'Yes'.lower():
            start()
        else:
            print('Please enter Yes or No. Thank you!!')
            Play_Again()

    Play_Again()

start()
```

"Save and run your code," Jack instructed. "Play the game a few times. Well done! Now, read through your code again, line by line and figure out what each line does exactly. Everything in this code was data covered in this book!"

"Good job!" Erik yelled. "You made a working game. Now here is your challenge:

"1. Change the Player_1 and Player_2 names from Jack and Erik to names of our choosing.

"2. Make the game Elephant, Cat, Mouse instead!"

"Huh? Elephant, cat, mouse?" Jack asked.

"Yeah," Erik answered. "*Elephant* beats *cat*. *Cat* beats *mouse*. *Mouse* beats *elephant*."

"So, you want them to change their code so that *rock* is *elephant*, *paper* is *mouse*, and *scissors* is *cat* or something?"

"Exactly."

"I've never heard of that game but it sounds like an interesting idea! Go for it!"

As the reader customized their program, an elephant walked into The Tech Academy. Jack and Erik were terrified as the elephant stomped towards them. Then suddenly, just as the reader completed their challenge, a mouse ran out, jumped up and ate a piece of cheese that was stuck to Erik's beard! The elephant trumpeted in terror and ran out of the room.

A cat chased the mouse away and everything returned to normal. Well, as normal as things can be when Jack and Erik are involved.

"Well, Erik," Jack began. "Our incredible reader has done it again. Another challenge completed successfully."

"I know!" Erik announced. "It's so sad that the next chapter is the last coding assignment."

"There, there, Erik. We will have other books for the reader."

"You're right. Now let's make a hangman game in Python!"

CHAPTER SEVENTEEN
HANGMAN

Erik stood alone on the top of Mount Everest. The sun was setting as he scratched behind the ears of an albino sasquatch. "Oh, Betty Sue," Erik sighed, "I am going to miss the reader."

"Arrgghhh! Shhhraaaamuuuuk!" Betty Sue, the great white sasquatch, roared in agreement.

Jack parachuted down and landed several feet away. He had never felt very comfortable around Betty Sue – even though she was a vegan.

"Erik," Jack pleaded. "I know it's sad but the book can't go on forever. Besides, we are going to make another cool game in Python!"

"Alright, alright," Erik answered. "But first, Betty Sue and I need to finish dinner."

Erik and Betty Sue chewed on random plants – a tree, grass, and a bush that Erik sometimes liked to hide behind when he was feeling scared. Jack ate a pepperoni pizza that he had in his backpack.

Once everyone was full, Betty Sue shouted, "Mooonnngeeeessoooo – kuuurrraaaakkkk!" and stomped off into her cave. Jack and Erik walked into a teleporter that was nearby and teleported back to The Tech Academy.

"Well, dear reader," Jack began, "we have grown close to you over these many chapters. And we've now come to the final program we will write in this book. It's been a long and interesting journey and we want to thank you for putting up with us."

Erik said, "Let's start our program by creating a New File in the text editor, and naming it hangman.py. Save hangman.py on your desktop. Then within the text editor, write the following code:"

```python
Name = input('Please enter the name of the person who created this game: ')
print('This game was made by the amazing ' + Name + '!')
print('Welcome to my guessing game!')
print('In this program, you will try to guess a word that I chose.')
print('Good luck!')
```

```python
def start():
    Player_Name = input('What is the name of the player? ')
    print('Greetings, ' + Player_Name + '! It is time to guess!')
    Secret_Word = 'ostrich'
    Guesses = ''
    Turns_Left = 11
    while Turns_Left > 0:
        Wrong_Answers = 0
        for Letter in Secret_Word:
            if Letter in Guesses:
                print(Letter)
            else:
                print('_')
                Wrong_Answers += 1
        if Wrong_Answers == 0:
            print('YOU WIN! You guessed my word: ' + Secret_Word + '!!!!!')
            break
        Guess = input('Guess a letter here: ').lower()
        Guesses += Guess

        if Guess not in Secret_Word:
            Turns_Left -=1
            print('Oops! This letter is not in my word. Please try again.')
            print('You have ' + str(Turns_Left) + ' more guesses left. You can do it!')
            if Turns_Left == 0:
                print('GAME OVER')

    def Play_Again():
        Again = input('Would you like to play again? ').lower()
        if Again == 'No'.lower():
            quit()
        if Again == 'Yes'.lower():
            start()
        else:
            print('Please enter Yes or No. Thank you!')
            Play_Again()

    Play_Again()

start()
```

"Save and run your code," Erik instructed. "You should have a friend or family member play the game to try to guess your secret word!"

"Now, it's time for the final challenge," Jack said. "Do the following:

"1. Change the secret word.

"2. Change the number of guesses allowed in your program."

Jack and Erik simply stared as the reader completed the challenge. "You know, Jack." Erik said. "I thought I'd be used to it by now, but the reader of this book continues to surprise me."

"They never cease to amaze," Jack agreed.

"I'm not good at long goodbyes."

"Me either. And let's not say goodbye. Let's say, 'Until next time.'"

"Yeah, we will see you again soon!"

"Thank you, reader, for showing us what a true coder is like. You're a special person!"

Jack tied a saddle to the back of a giant turtle, while Erik sat on Sally the ostrich's back. They looked at the reader one last time, gave a happy wave, and then rode their animals off into the sunset.

THE END
(FOR NOW...)

EPILOGUE

You have completed our book! Well done on your hard work and persistence!

You should now have a basic understanding of Python and coding.

If you're a kid or young adult, you can check out The Tech Academy's products and services here: learncodinganywhere.com

If you're a grown up, as the next step, we recommend enrolling in a Tech Academy coding boot camp. Our coding boot camps were designed like this book: for beginners and assuming no prior knowledge or experience.

Here are some of the reasons thousands of students have chosen to enroll at The Tech Academy:

1) Our curriculum – it's modern, robust (strong; holds up over time), and covers in-demand technologies. Our programs are thorough and cover more than just 1-2 languages. Our comprehensive curriculum ensures that students aren't pigeon-holed (restricted to an exclusive category) within a small skillset. Understanding a large array of technologies not only prepares graduates for the workforce, it assists them greatly in picking up new tech skills in the future.

2) We price our boot camps affordably. In fact, our tuition is less than the national average weekly cost of coding boot camps.

3) We require no technical background or experience. You don't have to already know coding to learn to code. As long as students can read, write and perform basic math, they can succeed at The Tech Academy.

4) We have a stellar online presence. Our average review rating across the top review sites ranges from 4.5-4.9 stars. We have received the Best Coding Boot Camp award several years in a row from SwitchUp.Org and CourseReport.Com (the top two boot camp review sites) and are included on several other top coding boot camp lists as well. We were also chosen as "The World's Best Code School" by the television show "World's Greatest." All of these awards and reviews are based on feedback from students and graduates of our programs.

5) We are extremely flexible. Students choose their own study schedule. They can study from home, at one of our campuses or both. They have online access to their program 24 hours a day. This ensures that students can enroll regardless of their life circumstances. The fact that the programs are self-paced is an aspect of our flexibility – students can blast through content they know well already, and take their time with new concepts. An additional factor in our flexibility is that we offer open enrollment, which means students can start anytime.

6) Our admissions staff and enrollment process are transparent and helpful. We answer questions and are polite, giving students a positive experience from the start.

To get started, visit The Tech Academy's website: learncodinganywhere.com

INDEX

!=, 73
>=, 73
<=, 73
==, 69
>>>, 45
Addition, 52
Case-sensitive, 60
Code
    definition, 24
Coding, 22
Computer
    definition, 10
Computer
programmer
    definition, 22
Concatenate
    definition, 54
    strings, 54
Counter, 86
"def", 112
Delete, 125
Developer
    definition, 22
Dictionaries, 105
Division, 54
Elif Statements, 77
Else Statements, 79
Equal to (==), 69

Float variable, 122
Function
    "def", 112
    definition, 111
    delete, 125
    length, 124
    input, 131
    round, 124
    .sort(), 140
    .split(), 116
    .swapcase(), 117
    .time.sleep(), 98
Greater Than or
Equal to (>=), 73
Hardware
definition, 20
IDLE, 40
If statements, 76
Indent, 78
Input
    definition, 15
    function, 131
Installation, 37
Integer
    definition, 124
    function, 124
Iteration, 100
Key, 106

Length function,
124
Less Than or Equal
to, (<=), 73
Lists, 83
    loops and lists,
101
Loop
    example, 95
    for loop, 99
    while loop, 95
Machine
    definition, 9
Mathematics
    addition, 52
    division, 54
    integer, 124
    operators, 53
    multiplication, 53
    subtraction, 53
Module
    definition, 90
    examples, 91
    import, 90
Multiplication, 53
Not Equal to, 73
Operators, 53
Parameter, 106

INDEX

Program
    definition, 19
Programmer
    definition, 22
Programming
Language
    definition, 26
Python
    case-sensitive,
60
    G. van Rossum, 31
    "hello, world", 45
    Installation, 37
    math, 51
    Monty Python, 32
Return, 32
Round Function,
124
Shell
    definition, 40
    example, 41
Software
definition, 20
.sort(), 140
.split(), 116
String variable
    concatenation,
54

    definition, 48
    example, 49
Subprogram
    definition, 114
    example, 113
Subtraction, 53
.swapcase(), 117
Syntax, 46
Text Editor, 41
time.sleep(), 98
Variables
    definition, 58
    example, 58

OTHER READING

Be sure to check out other Tech Academy books, which are all available for purchase on Amazon:

Learn Coding Basics in Hours with Small Basic

Programming for Absolute Beginners

Written by: Jack C. Stanley & Erik D. Gross,
Co-Founders of The Tech Academy

Learn Coding Basics in Hours with Python

Programming for Absolute Beginners

Written by: Jack C. Stanley & Erik D. Gross,
Co-Founders of The Tech Academy

LEARN CODING BASICS
IN HOURS
WITH JAVASCRIPT

Programming for Absolute Beginners

Written by: Jack C. Stanley & Erik D. Gross,
Co-Founders of The Tech Academy

PROJECT MANAGEMENT

HANDBOOK

Simplified Agile, Scrum and DevOps for Beginners

Written by
Jack C. Stanley & Erik D. Gross
Co-Founders of The Tech Academy

Made in the USA
Monee, IL
08 September 2020

(C)LEAN MESSAGING

A FRAMEWORK TO HELP STARTUP FOUNDERS TALK TO HUMANS

Scott Brown

None of this would be possible without the support of Wendy, Emmett & Elysha. Thank you.

CONTENTS

Warning 1

Introduction 3

What Are You Working On These Days? 10

Why Messaging is Important 25

The (C)lean Messaging Framework 37

Something About Them 43

Something About You 51

The (C)lean Message 54

A Simple Story 70

People Don't Remember Stats 75

Earworms 82

The Final Canvas 89

(C)lean Messaging in Conversation 93

You Need More Than One 111

Startup Examples 115

Conclusion 137

About the Author 142

Warning

Dear Reader,

Before we continue and dig into the mechanics of building your (C)lean Message, I want to warn you that this framework can be very powerful when applied to *any* idea.

If you use this framework, it's possible to craft a message that will resonate with potential customers and investors quickly. While this is a goal for most of us, a person could use this framework when the core fundamentals of the business are flawed, and still achieve results.

(C)lean Messaging

Do not lie. Do not be evil.

(C)lean messaging is a framework that will help startup founders talk to humans.   More importantly, it is a framework that will allow you to gain trust and agreement quickly.

Trust is fragile and valuable. Don't break it. Ever.

Sincerely,

Scott

Introduction

People have always told me "no."

Many years before I started my first company, I was an actor. During those years, I figured out that I would have to audition at least 40 times before I would get a role. That was 39 times that someone told me I sucked before one person would take a chance on me.

As an actor, the work can sometimes be deeply personal. So the risks you take in trying something new can feel like the worst fever dreams of youth. Remember those dreams about standing in front of your class naked? Every audition and every unusual choice in rehearsal can feel that way.

When the work is deeply personal and risky, and the ratio of no to yes is skewed heavily in favors of the "no's," it is a struggle. Moreover, because the need to share can be so fundamental to an actor, they push forward regardless of the fear and rejection.

The constant flurry of "no," helped me build up a tolerance to the word. More than a tolerance. Over the past 40-odd years, I have learned to look for the "no" and embrace the lessons it may carry.

I have been lucky enough to start nine companies since those early days on stage. I've had some very nice wins among those nine, and some failure as well. The wins have given me the freedom to share my learning along the way, and the failures have taught me lessons you can only learn in the darkest of times.

The one thing that ties a life on stage with life as an entrepreneur is the ability to break the power that "no" holds on us.

As a startup founder, you may have a great idea that is going to change the world, but when you hit the road to raise venture capital for the first time, it is virtually certain that ninety-nine people will say "no" before you find that one true believer who will fund your company.

Those odds are **twice as bad** as being an actor.

What we all learn as actors and entrepreneurs is that every "no" is a chance to perfect your craft and find another path toward yes.

During my career as a startup founder, I started to find some tools that would help me explain the innovation behind the business I was creating. At first, they were simple habits and rules of thumb that I would apply to a slide deck or presentation. I was lucky to have many opportunities to hear people tell me "no" along the way, and each one of those "no's" would help me craft a better message.

Like many startup founders, I would track the things that were working, and try to understand why. In many cases, the why behind some of it is still elusive, but the results are concrete.

Over the past few years, I have been fortunate to share some of the learnings I had gathered with other startup founders as both an active angel investor and advisor. I'll typically talk to 10-20 founders per week, and too often, I see the same challenges cropping up for many of them.

Startup founders are building amazing companies every day. However, the cognitive load placed on those hearing the pitch for the first time is unbearable. Founders make it far too hard for other people to understand their innovation quickly. This lack of understanding by the listener results in a tragically low success rate when the founder is selling to customers and investors. A customer will never buy something they do not understand. Moreover, they will not spend the energy to learn more if they do not see an immediate upside. When you have a limited financial runway, mean time to "yes" is a specter watching over you.

As founders, we have more tools than ever that will help us build a great business.

The frameworks, introduced in the last ten years that help founders build, measure & iterate their way toward product/market fit have been a lifesaver. Savvy founders use these tools and are far more likely to create something people might want to buy.

(C)lean Messaging

Surprisingly, the statistics around startup failure are the same as they were before those tools existed. We are building better companies, but we continue to suck at telling other people about them.

That's why I decided to release (C)lean Messaging to the world. (C)lean Messaging is a framework that helps startup founders talk to humans. By working in the familiar startup canvas model, a founder can build upon the work they've done to craft the business, but now have a tool to help them craft the message.

Hundreds of startups around the world have been introduced to (C)lean Messaging over the past few years and are seeing the immediate results. As a founder, your job is to communicate the vision and strategy of your company, and this new framework will help you do that faster/better -- dramatically decreasing your mean time to "yes."

Scott Brown

Getting people to understand the brilliance of your company is hard. You are not alone. 148,000 new technology startups are founded every month. The truth is that 90% of those companies will shut down before their first anniversary. You now have the chance to flip the narrative. Using (C)lean Messaging as the framework for how you talk about your idea, will reduce the time it takes for your potential customers, investors, and employees to say "yes."

Hearing "no" is great for learning, but hearing "yes" is better for business.

CHAPTER ONE

What Are You Working On These Days?

Tell me if this sounds familiar:

"So, whatcha ya workin' on these days?"

I know for me, I hear this simple question a dozen times each week. If I am honest, I ask that question even more! In a healthy startup ecosystem, everyone is both eager to help and looking to discover the next fantastic company. It's only natural. People love a good story and are hoping to learn something new or uncover an opportunity.

Now imagine you are hanging out at one of these startup events, lingering near the bar. The woman next to you is busily cranking away on her phone sending text messages faster than the guy behind the bar can pour pints of craft beer. As she puts her phone away, you turn to ask that default question: "So, what are you working on these days?"

"I have a startup that puts CRISPR on the blockchain, but using smart contracts, cuz all the MongoDB backend stuff won't scale. How about you?" She says.

After a quick sip of your beer, you say, "You know all those leaves we rake up into bags in the fall? If you own a house, my company leaf.ly can turn those bags of dead leaves into free money for you".

(C)lean Messaging

If you were a fly on the wall listening to these two, which story will prompt you to learn more?

Like most people, you are more likely to gravitate toward this crazy idea of turning leaves into money. I am sure our new friend with the CRISPR/blockchain/Smart Contract company is cool, but unless you already know what those things are, and why it matters to the world, the cognitive load on the listener is overwhelming. The listener is going to burn cycles and calories just trying to piece together what our friend said. If the listener does expend the energy to sort it out, it's hard to imagine they are going to remember it ten minutes later.

Building a company is hard. Even with all the smart tools, frameworks and blog posts with helpful advice, it takes extraordinary people like you to manifest something in spite of the uncertain outcome. Like most entrepreneurs, we focus our energy on validating what we learn, in order to find that elusive product/market fit.

You may have built a machine that turns trash bags of dead leaves into gold, but to get there, you had to invest time and energy doing amazing science. That science is hard, and you should be very proud of it. As a scientist, you probably didn't invent the "leaf-to-gold" process, you probably invented and patented a "mechanical system that ingests biological detritus in sufficient quantities, applies a bio-chemical gene splicing technology first invented during your PhD work at Stanford, that gradually manipulates the chemical bonds of the electrons in the source material so that the output is more closely aligned with group 11 elements; while specifically targeting an atomic number that approaches 79 with consistency."

Don't get me wrong, the science is compelling, and that founder should be celebrated for turning ancient alchemy into something real. The challenge is that unless ordinary people invest significant time to experience or understand it, no one is going to care. And it will be near impossible for the press to write about it. Believe me, you will get a lot of coverage in the scientific journals, but you won't see this story on the evening news where it belongs.

STANDING ON THE SHOULDERS OF GIANTS

Today, the concepts behind The Lean Startup seems obvious to an entrepreneur.

In the world of the modern startup, we have absorbed the practice Eric Ries defined back in 2008. There isn't a founder in the world today that doesn't talk about minimum viable products, pivots, falsifiable hypotheses, Build -> Measure -> Iterate & validated learning.

Scott Brown

The Lean Startup approach changed the world.

Around the same time, Alex Osterwalder had released his first business modeling tool to document and digest a company business model. The Business Model Canvas was a breakthrough in the toolsets for a modern startup. Since 2008, the Business Model Canvas has been modified and adjusted to focus on particular aspects of an industry or type of company. The Lean Canvas by Ash Maurya is an example of the Business Model Canvas with a focus on early-stage startup development. The Lean Canvas approach tightly aligned the language of Lean Startup with a framework for launching a technology startup.

As founders, this changed the game for us. By following the simple principles brought forth in these books and tools, we all got out of the office to speak with potential customers. We were in the struggle with customers by following the process of building, testing, and tweaking our idea based on what we learned. As we validated our learning, we tracked our progress using some form of business model canvas.

I credit these frameworks for the global democratization of entrepreneurship we have seen over the past ten years. With just a little understanding of the process and the frameworks, anyone could start a company and start building a product that people might want.

Of course, there is always a gap.

While the Lean Canvas placed a strong focus on helping a founder figure out *what* to build, founders still had trouble defining for *whom* they were building the product.

Along came Mr. Osterwalder, again.

Alex saw the same gap in the system and built a new canvas he called the Value Proposition Canvas. The Value Proposition Canvas was a lifesaver for many of us. It built off the foundations created in a founder's Lean Canvas or Business Model Canvas, but with a focus on helping us figure out "the who" in our business model.

Who has real pain? Who has the most to gain? What features and benefits have we validated that can solve for those pains and gains? Again, Alex was able to influence the next wave of entrepreneurs and help us all narrow in on the customers that would most benefit from our products.

With all of these tools at our disposal, naturally, we have cracked the nut on how to build a startup, right? I wish that were true.

We all know the statistics when it comes to building a startup. 90% of the companies created this year are going to shut down before they hit their one-year anniversary. That's brutal! Even with all these tools at our disposal, the rate of failure remains the same as it was when I started my first company in 1993.

Recently, the online research firm CBInsights did a study to figure out why these numbers were still so high. In their research, they found that 42% of founders after they shut down, said they had to close the doors because there was no "market fit." How could this be true? If founders are all using the tools, and if we are all standing on the shoulders of these startup giants, how is it that anyone builds something that doesn't have a market?

I have been lucky to work with hundreds of founders over the years, and I have never met one that thought they were building a product that didn't have a market. However, it seems like a convenient factor to blame after the fact.

I believe the problem is not *market fit*; it's *market framing*.

MARKET FRAMING IS THE REAL PROBLEM

In the new model of startup development, we talk about customer discovery and a validated learning loop based on the Lean Startup Process and validating our value proposition using the tools that Alex introduced.

Here is the thing, especially as technical founders, we leverage all this stuff and it increases our odds of building the right thing for the right people. What it doesn't do, is help us talk to people about what we have created.

Talking with humans is the next gap in our startup toolkit.

(C)lean Messaging

At some point, every startup has to stop doing "customer discovery" and start talking to potential investors, future customers, and the media. Too often, our humble founders are not prepared for those conversations. They introduce too much cognitive load for their listener, and in the end, lose deals because the person across the table just doesn't get it.

Market fit was never the problem. The problem is that founders have not had the tools to help them talk to actual humans.

Over the years, when I sat down with founders, I saw this same issue over and over again. Founders would typically fall into two groups: Mr. Recipe or Ms. Lookatme. Let's look at how each of these founders would describe their new fictional cookie company, called Qookie.

When you ask Mr. Recipe what they are working on, he is likely to say:

> "At Qookie, we sell small cakes made from stiff, sweet dough rolled and sliced or dropped by the spoonful on a large, flat pan and baked."

While this is entirely accurate, it isn't what a customer needs to know about Qookie. This pitch is the exact stuff you need to know in order to *duplicate* their business. It's the recipe.

Explaining how to duplicate a business happens all the time, and it's easy to fall into this trap. Remember, as the founder, Mr. Recipe spent months interviewing customers and learning what they need/want to solve their cookie problem. He may have done dozens of interviews with potential customers and learned all the features needed to satisfy the market. Then when Mr. Recipe meets his first set of real potential customers, he knows that all the stuff he built is essential to solving a person's problem and so all he does is repeat the list of things he had to do to build the business.

Giving people the recipe will work sometimes, but not at scale, and certainly not at the speed needed to gain customers faster than Mr. Recipe will spend money.

Ms. Lookatme has a different approach. She knows that she needs to find an angle and marketing message for Qookie. So, when you ask her about Qookie she will say something like:

> "At Qookie, we sell portable desserts in convenient packs of 12!"

Again, this is absolutely true. The problem is that it's all about Qookie. Here's the thing, when you are telling someone about your business, it is not about you.

The person who asked, "what are you working on these days?" is actually asking you "what are you working on that could benefit me?".

When Ms. Lookatme talks about the business, she frames it about her. It is about *what* the business does, and not the problem they are solving, or the people they are helping, or how Qookie can change the life of the listener.

When a person hears Mr. Recipe for the first time, they have to hear all those words, then figure out what problem that recipe will solve, and then if that problem is big enough to care about solving it.

When a person hears Ms. Lookatme for the first time, the listener is stuck trying to figure out if what Ms. Lookatme does matters to them at all.

In both cases, our founders are building a mental hurdle that the listener needs to jump before they can engage. The more technical or complex your business, the more significant the mental barrier. The truth is that humans are lazy! So, if you are making people work to understand your business, you have already lost.

Startup founders have solved the challenge of what to build and for whom to build a product. The challenge we are left with is talking about what we have built to actual people. That's why, after years of mentoring startups, I've created a new framework called (C)lean Messaging, that will help you talk to humans about the cool thing you've invented.

Talking to real people about your company is hard, but you are not alone.

CHAPTER TWO

Why Messaging is Important

If you can't talk about it, how do you expect to sell it?

Startup founders are unquestionably the experts on their business. They know the science and their product to a depth that most people will never achieve. A founders expertise is an advantage in the building process, but it's a liability when it comes to sharing the idea with the world.

Often you hear people ask a founder to simplify the story, or "Explain like I'm 5 years old". When someone has a mountain of knowledge, it is difficult to bring the story down to eye level for the average listener.

I am always reminded of that great quote from Albert Einstein, "If you can't explain it simply, you don't understand it well enough."

You have done the work to build a real business, but with the massive amount of competition for brain space in your customers' head, if you cannot find a way to present your company with simplicity and clarity, you are doomed.

Fred Wilson, from Union Square Ventures, famously laid out the three things that all startup CEOs need to do. It's the roadmap for the role of CEO and resonates for many of us.

- Set the overall vision and strategy of the company and communicates it to all stakeholders

- Recruit, hire, and retain the very best talent for the company
- Make sure there is always enough cash in the bank

This is excellent stuff, but too often we skip right over that critical word "communicate" in the first principle. As a startup founder, you get to set the vision and strategy, but it is critical that you **communicate** it to your stakeholders as well.

In a simple world, it is easy to think that stakeholders are your employees, investors, and customers. We do not live in a simple world.

Your stakeholders today are everywhere.

Your employees, investors, and customers are clearly stakeholders. To build a scalable company today, you need to embrace a broader definition that includes the community, your family, and the media.

If you embrace the broader view of communicating to stakeholders, you will start to build a following of people that can share and expand the reach of your company story. The easier it is for people to share your story, the faster it will travel in the community.

There are four critical moments for a founder when they are asked to talk about their business. I call it the four P's of the startup apocalypse.

- The **Party**
- The **Pitch**
- The **Press**
- The **People**

Every one of these moments can make or break your company. It's in these moments that you can supercharge your business with (C)lean Messaging.

THE PARTY

Dinner parties. Cocktail hours. A mingle. Conference networking. Hanging out on the playground while you wait for the bell to ring at your daughters' school.

Where are the places when you get the random question about what you do for a living? For many of us, these events are like going to the dentist. We have to do it, but there are one hundred other places we would all rather be.

It doesn't matter if it's a work event or a social event, someone is going to ask what you do for a living. And not surprisingly, these casual encounters can often lead to new opportunity. Maybe the person you meet at that cocktail hour is a venture capitalist that is looking for the next big thing.

(C)lean Messaging

That sinking feeling in your stomach when you show up at one of these things is a physical manifestation of our collective dread of small talk.

The secret to crushing a conference networking event is to make sure that you are not the only one telling your story. We all struggle to find topics of discussion at these things, so if you make your company message interesting, simple, and repeatable, every person you talk with is more likely to share the story with the next group.

A (C)lean Message will spread like wildfire through a party.

THE PITCH

We all have to pitch.

Between the founding of startup two and three for me, I joined a small company as one of three salespeople. For a couple of years, I carried a bag and a quota. There is nothing quite like having your paycheck depend on your ability to sell. It will teach you as much about yourself as it does the craft of selling.

As a founder, you are the best salesperson in the company. No one knows your product the way you do. So naturally, when the time comes, you will get the call to give the big pitch. Will you be ready?

Modern sales strategy is more about relationships, empathy, and curiosity. However, we know that every sales meeting starts with a simple pitch on the business. To be honest, the pitch is happening from both sides of the table. The sales person is introducing their company, and the customer is selling themselves to position for a better deal. Most experts agree that the sale is won or lost in those first few minutes. So, you better make it easy for the other side to understand your business.

(C)lean Messaging

For startups, you are going to be asked to pitch all the time. It might be a demo day event in front of hundreds of people or standing up to pitch a team of investors. The pitch is your moment to influence the entire audience. However, if you make it too hard for them, they will tune out and start checking their phone. If you have ever stood up in a room to pitch and saw all those blue faces from the light on their screens, you know the frustration.

Doing a big pitch like that can be tough for a startup founder. 75% of people on the planet say that their number one fear in life is public speaking. Death is all the way down at number four! It reminds me of that old Jerry Seinfeld joke:

> "People would rather be the guy in the casket, than the guy giving the eulogy!"

Try to remember that a pitch is a bridging event to a more in-depth conversation. The trick here is being able to convince someone, in a very big room, that they should spend their valuable time having that deeper conversation with you.

THE PRESS

There is nothing better than a face to face conversation with a potential customer. That may work for your first 50 customers. Eventually, you will need to leverage outside media to share your story if you want to scale.

Today, there are more media outlets than ever before. For a startup founder, your job is to help each of those media outlets deliver value to their customers. So, who are the customers exactly? The details depend on the outlet, but it is important to remember that a writer, podcaster, television journalist is looking to share interesting content with their audience. The more interesting it is, and the easier it is for the audience to understand, the more likely they will be to return for more content.

When you are speaking with a reporter, remember that you are actually speaking with their audience. Your job is to make it easy for the reporter to craft a story that will garner clicks and attention.

Every reporter is looking for a hook. A simple, clear message that that can lead the story and hook the reader into spending their time to read the article. As a startup founder, if you show up well prepared, you are more likely to get a great article written.

There is very little difference between reporters, bloggers, and podcasters these days. They all are looking to build their audience using content you help them create. The challenge for a startup founder is hooking the reporter.

Remember that you are not alone in your goal of getting press exposure, and there are thousands of other startups struggling to get that same space. If you are creating an additional cognitive load for the writer, they have many other stories they can write, and they will move on.

THE PEOPLE

Your biggest asset as a startup founder is the people you assemble around you. Your first job as a startup founder is to build the team. Easier said than done.

In the early days of a startup, the only tool you have to recruit a world-class team is the story of the business. And again, this is make-or-break time. Your story is what will capture the imagination of smart people who want to help.

(C)lean Messaging

Very few people ever joined a company because they use Blockchain. However, many people join companies to change the world or because they believe in the mission of the founders.

Remember what Fred Wilson said about the job of a startup CEO? His second principle was to recruit and hire the very best people. So, when you sit down with a potential new hire, will they walk away inspired or just walk away?

CHAPTER THREE

The (C)lean Messaging Framework

WARNING

STOP.

Before we continue and dig into the mechanics of building your (C)lean Message, I want to warn you again, that this framework can be very powerful when applied to *any* idea.

If you use this framework, it's possible to craft a message that will resonate with potential customers and investors quickly. While this is a goal for most of us, a person could use this framework when the core fundamentals of the business are flawed, and still achieve results.

Do not lie. Do not be evil.

OVERVIEW

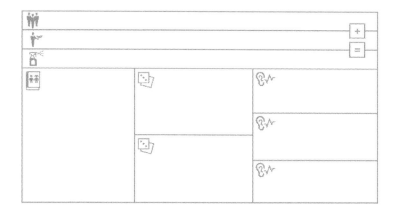

When Archimedes was demonstrating the principles of the lever, he said, "Give me a place to stand, and I shall move the world!".

With (C)lean Messaging, I hope to give you a place to stand when you are talking about your company or idea.

The (C)lean Messaging framework has been developed over the past few years and is designed to build upon the success of the Business Model Canvas, Lean Startup Canvas, and Value Proposition Canvas. Anyone with an idea should be able to use these tools to build the right thing, for the right people, and when combined with (C)lean Messaging they will be able to talk to the world about it.

Before we begin, you should download a copy of the framework to review and practice while we review each section.

(C)lean Messaging

http://CleanMessaging.co/canvas

Remember to sign up for the (C)lean Messaging newsletter, to get updates and hear stories of other startup founders using this framework to grow their business. I promise never to sell or share your information and will respect your communication preferences.

To see what others are doing with (C)lean Messaging, search Twitter for the hashtag #cleanmessaging and join the conversation.

THE CANVAS

In the following chapters, we will break down every section of the (C)lean Messaging framework in detail. First, let's take a quick peek at the entire canvas.

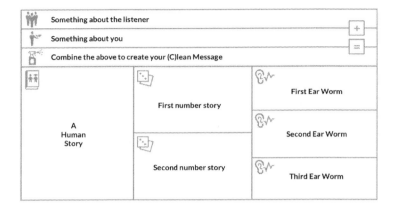

The (C)lean Messaging canvas will focus you first on the real human need of the listener. Once you know what the listener is hoping for, you narrow down your idea or product into one simple thing, the most important thing about your business. By combining those two elements, we will craft a (C)lean Message. You can think of this as the "poetry" of your business.

Now, that we have a (C)lean Message, we start to support that message with three parts: A human story, a couple of number analogies, and three memorable phrases that will help make your idea stick in your listeners' memory.

Let's dig deep on each of these sections to uncover the craft of building your (C)lean Message.

CHAPTER FOUR
Something About Them

It's no accident that (C)lean Messaging starts with the listener.

As a startup founder, it is imperative that you recognize one simple truth:

When you are telling
someone about your
company, it's no longer
about you.

You spent many hours thinking & building to get to this point when you can share your kickass idea with the world. But guess what, no one cares about the work you have done to get here.

As soon as you start talking, your job is to help the listener achieve _their_ goals. It is your ability to help the listener achieve their goals that will allow them to help you achieve yours.

If your listener believes that you are helping them achieve their goals, they will reward you by supporting your ask of them. Your "ask" may be buying a product, becoming a beta customer, investing in the company or joining your mission.

It is critical to remember that people will reward those who help them.

It is your job to provide the help.

Focusing on the listener can feel a little weird at first. For many startup founders, we will go into a conversation knowing that if this potential customer will buy our product, it's a massive help to our business. Alternatively, a founder will position themselves as needing an investor to help grow the business when the opposite is far more powerful.

Our first goal with (C)lean Messaging is to identify the thing that your listener most needs, wants or hopes for in the context of your business.

Let's say you have a business that is selling software to alert an engineer when an important computer server goes offline. When you sit down to talk to the Vice President of Engineering in a potential customers office, what is their deep human need?

Is it to get alerts when a server goes offline?

That may be the solution they need, but *why* do they want to be alerted when that critical infrastructure goes down? If you know someone in this type of role at a company, you know that they are always connected to their phone. Always on the watch for a potential problem.

What's it like to live that person's life?

Imagine the conversations she has with her spouse about "putting away the phone," or the frustration when they are called away from their child's ballgame to handle a work problem?

These are real, deep and human issues. Those are the real problems your potential customer wants to solve.

Often, I hear from founders that this makes sense for a consumer product, but what about when you are selling to the enterprise? Please remember that no one has ever sold something to a Fortune 100 company. However, many of us have sold to people who happen to work at a Fortune 100 company. You cannot sell to an address, there are always people you are talking with, and those people are making the buying decision.

Focus on the deep human needs of your listener. What do they crave, love, hate, fear, avoid, cherish or embrace?

Those human things are what will move your listener toward your idea.

When you fill in this section of the canvas, find the most human example of the need your listener will have. A strong answer to this part of the canvas will immediately resonate with people. It will make them say "Ah! No kidding. That is exactly my life...".

Bad: "People want alerts when servers go offline."

Good: "People want to leave their phone at home when they go on vacation."

You want this section to be immediately recognizable by the listener as a problem that they are likely to have experienced. Craft the problem as one that strikes right at the core of the listener.

Bad: "People want car tires to last more than 30,000 miles."

Good: "Buying tires make people feel like they are getting ripped off."

WHO IS THE LISTENER?

Sometimes it's easy to figure out who your "listener" is for your (C)lean Message.

If you are selling a product to office managers at small businesses, and those office managers can swipe a credit card to buy without consulting anyone else, it is pretty clear that a "sales" focused (C)lean Messaging canvas will have that office manager as the listener.

What about a more complex sale? The trick here is to narrow down your list of "possible" listeners to as few as possible. In an enterprise sale, you may have buyers and influencers, but they may have the same deep human need. Can you identify the most profound common human need for that group?

If you have a marketplace-style business, where there are two or more sides of the business, and you sit in the middle, it is likely that you will need a

(C)lean Messaging

(C)lean Message canvas that targets each side separately.

What about the media?

When you are talking to the press or any other online media (bloggers, podcasters, etc.) your listener is not the person with whom you are speaking. Your messaging focus should be on the audience of the reporter, not the reporter in front of you.

In those situations, try to think past your interviewer and focus your message on the people who will be listening or reading the content later.

CHAPTER FIVE

Something About You

What is the single most critical thing you solve?

Identifying the most critical thing you solve may seem easy, at first, but the more you think about it, the harder it becomes.

(C)lean Messaging

Boiling down your idea to one thing is tricky, but vital to your success.

As founders, we know that every part of the system we have built is essential. Otherwise, we wouldn't have spent all that time and money building it, right?

The trap here is that while all of those things are important, only one of them is critical to your core message *for this listener*!

Bad: "We send alerts, and monitor system processes, and track performance, and proactively scrub logs using our proprietary and patent-pending AI system designed by three Ph.D. candidates from Stanford."

Good: "We let you know when computer service is non-functional."

At this point in the process, it is ok to leave the language a little technical. In the next section, we will break it down so humans can understand. Right now, the focus should be on the single most important thing you do for your listener.

In the example above, you can see the problem. The dreaded "and" shows up everywhere. Hard to claim you have found the singularly most important thing if it is full of conjunctions.

If you see the word "and" or any other linking words/phrases, go back to work.

An excellent way to narrow in on that one big thing is to think about tomorrow for your listener. What is the one thing you want the listener to remember about you tomorrow? If nothing else, what is the critical thing you want them to know that you will do to help them?

CHAPTER SIX

The (C)lean Message

A (C)lean Message allows your listener to recall your vision of an uncertain future easily.

Imagine you had a key that would open 63% of locks in the world. That would be pretty cool, right?

As humans we all kind of suck at remembering things. With a few exceptions, we don't recall details of the discussions we might have had 10 minutes ago, let alone a discussion we had weeks ago. However, we do remember the way that we felt during that conversation. Emotions evolved in humans as a way to flag events in our mind. Think of it like flagging an email in your inbox.

With a (C)lean Message we are hacking that innate "feature" of the human brain to tag words with emotion and lock it into long-term memory in the brain of our listener.

When you get it right, your listener will remember your message more than 60% of the time. How cool is that?

Building a (C)lean Message starts with a simple formula:

Something about the listener

+   Something about you

=   A (C)lean Message

We start with the vital information about our listener and smash it together with the key thing we want that listener to know about your idea or business.

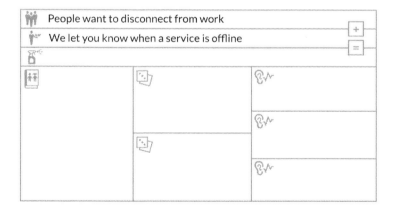

When we look at the example above, we know that people want a way to disconnect from work. That seems natural, and everyone who hears that would agree. Looking at the next bit about the business, "We let you know when a service is offline," again that is simple and absolutely true.

Our goal now is to smash those together into the poetry of your business. We always start with the listener's concern and then combine with the solution. So, a (C)lean Message for our fictional company could be something like:

People want to disconnect from work		+
We let you know when a service is offline		=
Leave your phone at home, because we have your back.		

(C)lean Messaging

Leave your phone at home, because we have your back.

That's pretty good. We start with the idea that a person like your listener can disconnect themselves from the office by leaving their phone at home.   And then follow up with why that is possible: we have your back.

A (C)lean message like this is simple, focused on the listener, small & easy to remember. You can imagine someone else describing this company as "the people that have my back so that I can leave my phone in the car during Jimmy's baseball game."

Getting this line right is hard. You will have to test it with people, try it out, see if it works. Be courageous and try something that seems too simple. We have found in practice that simple is usually better. There will always be time to expand on the idea and take a listener deeper into *how* you can solve the problem.

You will know you have a (C)lean Message when it's sharp as a SABER.

- **S**imple
- **A**udience-focused
- **B**ite-sized
- **E**ar worthy
- **R**epeatable

SIMPLE

It's hard to overstate the power of simplicity.

There's a reason why presidential speeches typically contain words in the grade eight to ten range. Everyday language is received as more trustworthy by a general audience. Concise, clear communication is most effective. The need for clarity is supported by an NYU study that explored the impact of abstract language versus concrete language on listeners. The study concluded what presidents know: a general audience of listeners will judge overly wordy or complicated language to be less trustworthy than simple, concrete speech.

And yet, startup founders are in love with jargon and acronyms.

For many founders, jargon is a shortcut to credibility or trust. In some cases that is true, but 99% of the time, jargon will do more damage than good. The only shortcut to trust - is clarity.

When you can describe your business using simple words, it shows that you know the content at a deeper level.

Highly technical founders often have a difficult time simplifying their speech, especially if they've been steeped in industry knowledge for a long time. What they consider basic knowledge may be jargon to a general audience. These founders are at risk of assuming their audience knows more about a given topic than they do.

This results in the last thing you want to create: a lack of clarity and a lack of trust.

Know that there is always an effective way to communicate an idea, to anyone - without overly technical language.

Even when the product you're creating is incredibly technical, complex, and confusing to explain, there is always a way to simplify. I encountered a situation like this recently while meeting with a founder I know who's spent the last five years building a fantastic technology. It's called a micro OLT, and, technically speaking, it's fabricated to push fiber deeper to extend the PON to low-power MDUs.

(C)lean Messaging

Now, I know a good bit about fiber networking and optical networks - but I still didn't know what any of that meant.

So, I told him to explain it to me like I was five years old.

Even then, there were still too many words. I knew there was a more straightforward way to get to the core of it. So, we boiled it down, then broke it down some more. Now he says: "We've built a tiny device that allows apartment building tenants to get ultra-fast internet at lower costs."

The difference is immense. Only a few people on earth would buy a micro OLT that pushes fiber deeper for MDUs. No one would know what that was! However, plenty of people would buy a device that lets them provide faster internet for more people at a lower cost.

Simplify, simplify, simplify.

The most effective, convincing use of language precisely communicates what you're saying in the fewest, simplest words. As French philosopher and mathematician Blaise Pascal once said, "I would have written a shorter letter, but I did not have time." On the same note, when then-President Woodrow Wilson was asked how long it took him to prepare for a speech, he replied, "If it is a ten-minute speech, it takes me all of two weeks to prepare it; if it is a half-hour speech it takes me a week; if I can talk as long as I want to, it requires no preparation. I am ready now."

Being clear and concise is difficult. However, when you are, it sends the message that you understand both the content and your listener.

AUDIENCE FOCUSED

(C)lean Messaging

Remember the fatal flaw of Ms. Lookatme?

When she was talking about her cookie company, it was all about her.

A good (C)lean Message starts with the listener. As a founder you have to remember that once you are talking to someone else, it is no longer about you, it is about what you can do for someone else.

What is the big problem you are trying to solve? What deep human struggles do your customers face every day?

In the theatre, they talk about how every character is the hero of their own story. Even the bad guys! It's vital to remember this because your customer is the hero of their story, not you. Your job is to show up with a way to help that potential customer on their hero journey. They are not considering your product with the goal of helping you meet your quarterly sales targets.

When you are crafting a (C)lean Message, focus on the listeners' needs first, then show how you can help.

BITE-SIZED

My wife and I love tapas.

Given a choice, we will seek out great tapas before a great steak every time.

It may be indecision on our part, but we love sampling a little bit of everything and enjoying a wide variety of flavors over a leisurely meal. Tapas are bite-sized and shareable.

Your (C)lean Messaging should be the same.

Think of this as the haiku of your business. Have you found the shortest possible way to say something, and still make it clear? Forcing yourself to be bite-sized will encourage you to trim out the excess details and focus on the most important things.

An easy way to look for a (C)lean Message that is leaning toward super-sized is to watch for the word "and." Anytime you see the word "and" it is likely that you are trying to string together many things to describe your business, rather than finding the single most important thing.

If you find yourself trying something like: "We are a floor wax and salad dressing and glass cleaner and sandwich spread...", first, you should question the business model. Second, you should look for the way to simply group those things. It makes me wonder if the real business we are talking about is an "edible cleaning solution"?

EAR WORTHY

How do you know if something is ear-worthy? It just sounds right.

Is it easy to say and repeat? Does the way you have it phrased feel good and easy to say?

Like good poetry, a strong (C)lean Message sounds right and feels good to hear. It may feel subjective, and in a way, it is probably. However, like other things in this world, you know it when you see it. Let's look at a few examples:

"We sell automobiles to foreign visitors on 3-month visitor visa's in the US."

- OR -

"We give long-term tourists the freedom of the open road."

(C)lean Messaging

They both say the same thing, but the second one just "sounds better," right? How about another?

"We free fickle teenagers from mobile phone fees."

- OR -

"We kill unexpected mobile fees."

The first one sounds like a tongue twister to me, while the second sounds interesting - I would want to learn more.

REPEATABLE

The most potent (C)lean Messages are ones that are easily repeatable.

It is this little bit of the puzzle that will allow your (C)lean Message to get viral traction in your community. If people love telling the story of your business, you get the exponential benefits.

If you think about it, people often buy things because they want to share the story of their purchase with someone else. Make sure your message is easy to repeat, and you will see a remarkable upside.

To be repeatable, you need to carefully craft your (C)lean Message so it will stick in the listeners' memory. If it is not memorable, there is no way people will repeat it to others.

CHAPTER SEVEN

A Simple Story

Humans are wired for story.

Since the beginning of human language, we have used stories to share experiences of the world. These stories were used to teach lessons to the audience about the environment, morality, opportunity, and more.

When we hear a story about a person just like us, the trials they went thru and the outcomes they had based on their decisions, we naturally put ourselves into the role of the hero. Our brains track the story and consider the choices the hero made, and it forces us to think about the choices we would make in a similar circumstance.

Now that we have a strong (C)lean Message, we need to support it with three key elements. The first of which is a human story where the listener could picture themselves as the hero.

For a startup founder, the first place to start may be the story of your first superstar customer. What happened to that first customer AFTER they used your product? Tell me about Sally, the single mom and VP of Engineering for Acme Corporation and what her life was like after buying your service.

(C)lean Messaging

Imagine a story like this:

"When we first met Sally, she was the VP of Engineering for Acme Corp, and she told us about the time her phone lit up with server issues while she was at her daughter's dance recital. She had to slip out the back of the room to deal with the issue and missed her daughter's big moment on stage. That is a moment she will never get back. After using our solution, she likes to say that she 'feels human again.' Like she can balance the important things in her life, along with her demanding career. Sally is crushing it at work, but more importantly, she knows she will never miss another moment with her family."

That is the kind of story that will resonate with your listeners. They will hear about Sally and remember all the times they had to skip out on an event or got stuck at the office during a family meal.

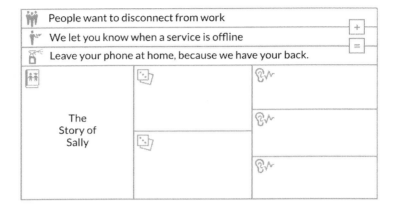

People want to disconnect from work		+
We let you know when a service is offline		=
Leave your phone at home, because we have your back.		

The story of Sally is used to support your (C)lean Message in conversation. It is the ultimate example of how your idea can change lives. Notice that the startup, the idea, and the features are not the center of the story. This story is all about Sally.

You want your listener to hear this story, picture themselves as Sally, and desire the future that she has now.

When you tell a story like this, the brain of the listener will do most of the work for you. Your

(C)lean Messaging

listener will automatically assume that Sally is a proxy for themselves, and their brain will fill in all the details on how your solution made Sally's (their!) life better.

CHAPTER EIGHT

People Don't Remember Stats

People don't remember numbers.   People remember the way numbers made them feel.

As a founder, your goal is to be remembered.

(C)lean Messaging

The average venture capitalist will meet dozens of startups every week, but they only remember a few of the companies. It is those few that are genuinely memorable that get the benefit of in-depth discussion at the Monday partner meetings.

At the same time, our business is measured in numbers. That's the rub.

A few years back the London School of Business did a study to gauge the long-term memory of data that was presented to a subject. The results were fascinating.

They found that if a person was presented with statistics on a topic, shortly afterward, the person could only recall about 5-10% of the information. Ouch.

When the statistics were paired with an image, the person was able to recall closer to 25% of the content. That's a nice improvement, over pure numbers!

Now here is the kicker. When the statistics were shared in the form of a story, retention increased to **over 65%**. The conclusion that the London School of Business made was that by engaging both the right and left sides of the brain, the subject retained more of the content in long-term memory.

The resulting application is pretty obvious.

We all have essential numbers about our business. They are important in understanding why what we are doing is going to change the world. If people don't remember those numbers, the numbers don't matter. Our goal is to frame the most important numbers in a story or analogy that will cement them into the long-term memory of the listener.

(C)lean Messaging

Let's think about an example. Today, there are 148,000 new tech startups founded every month around the world. That is a HUGE number. The number of new startups per month may be a critical number for your listener to understand, and grasp the size of the market or the scope of competition in the world today.

If I am on a podcast and say, "148,000 new startups are founded every month around the world", only about 5% of the listeners will remember that information. Because they won't remember it, the rest of my message is going to fall flat. Moreover, in the future, the listener will not be able to share with friends why my idea is going to change the world.

What if I were to lead with something like this?

"Every time a baby is born in Amsterdam, a new tech startup is launched somewhere in the world."

Dang. That will stick.

I have been using this statistic on stage for a couple of years, and I cannot count the number of times I now hear other people use it in their presentations. The idea that mothers in Amsterdam are delivering little startups at the same rate as their little bundle of joy is going to hit that long-term memory, every time.

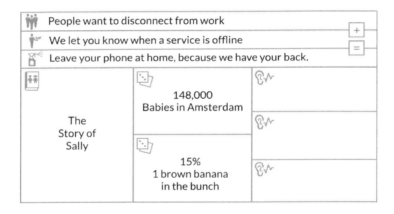

In this section of the (C)lean Messaging framework, our goal is to identify the two key numbers that a listener MUST remember for the rest of our story to make sense. In any business, there are a few numbers that will mater. Some examples include:

- The size of the market
- The number of resources available
- The number of customers you have
- The time you have been working on the problem
- Traction
- Scope
- Opportunity
- Scale

You should figure out those two most critical numbers, then frame them in an analogy. Imagine it's critical that your listener remember that 15% of employees are not engaged at work. To get that to stick you might have a number story about bananas. "Imagine if every time you bought a bunch of bananas, one of them was already brown and squishy."

Statistic: 15% of employees are not engaged at work

Number story: Imagine if every time you bought a bunch of bananas, one of them was already brown & squishy. That's what it's like in your office right now. About 1 out of every 7 people in the office are not engaged with their work.

Your listener may never remember that 15% of people are disengaged, but they will remember that in a bunch of bananas, one of them is brown & squishy. The phrase "brown & squishy" becomes synonymous with a disengaged employee.

In this framework, you need to find two of these great number stories. Make them relevant and stick in your listener's long-term memory by giving it context and color.

CHAPTER NINE

Earworms

I am sure you have all heard someone tell you that the human attention span is less than the attention span of a goldfish.

That is a lie.

The truth is that our attention span isn't shorter, it is just that we have a lot more competition for our attention these days.

The key to being heard in this noisy world is to give away ear candy like it is Halloween every day.

The internet economy runs on the back of catchy phrases that drive viewers and clicks. The more viewers & clicks an article receives, the more advertising dollars for the media outlet. That audience engagement is what determines success for the writer. Which in turn creates success for you, and for the media properties that want to write about you.

Your job as a founder is to make it easier for the media to gain clicks and views, while at the same time, making it easy for people listening to share your story with others.

(C)lean Messaging

That is where the mighty "earworm" comes into play.

In the (C)lean Messaging canvas, we want to find three great, catchy phrases that can become the "click-bait" for your business.

Imagine the best headline you could ever hope for about your business?

- "Company X turns acorns into gold."
- "Company Y gives you the freedom to think again."
- "Company Z will pay you to sleep late on Sundays."

These are all great examples of headlines that start from the work we do in this section of the canvas. Find the short, memorable and catchy phrases you can use to highlight some aspect of your business. It doesn't have to describe *everything* you do, just some *critical element* that will make people want to learn more.

A great way to test something in this section is as an answer to those dinner party questions about what you do for a living.

Guest: What do you do for a living?

Me: I have a little company that **turns acorns into gold**.

Guest: Damn! Tell me more!

(C)lean Messaging

If you hear that powerful little phrase "tell me more," you know you have a winner.

When you build three of these phrases in the framework, you are giving your listener easy ways to share your story and giving the media easy ways to write a clickable headline. If your story has more audience engagement than other things they have written, that writer is going to keep coming back for more stories. Make sense?

The great thing about these "earworms" is that they are the seeds to the viral growth of your story. If you land a few winners in this section, your listener is going to spread your story, because it is too much fun to pass up.

Same dinner party:

Guest: Hey, have you met Scott? He has this little company that **turns acorns into gold**!
 Other Guest: No way?!? I gotta meet that guy...

Me: <mic drop>

SECRET WEAPON

Here is a little trick you can try with this section. Make your earworm a wordplay on some well-known idiom. Because those old tropes are so ingrained in our memory already, your version gets the advantage of that well-worn path in the brain.

Making your message stick in long-term memory faster and with less work.

Why is that important? A founder's job is to be remembered.

- An acorn in hand is worth two bucks in your wallet.
- The only things certain in life are death, taxes, & servers going down while you are on vacation

(C)lean Messaging

- Take my WiFi. Please.

CHAPTER TEN
The Final Canvas

People want to disconnect from work		+
We let you know when a service is offline		=
Leave your phone at home, because we have your back.		
The Story of Sally	148,000 Babies in Amsterdam	We turn server alerts into lemonade
	15% 1 brown banana in the bunch	We don't sell dashboards, we sell Sundays with family
		Alerts are for chumps

Voila!

Our first (C)lean Messaging canvas is complete for our server management company.

(C)lean Messaging

Something About Them:

People want to disconnect from work

Something About You:

We let you know when a service goes offline

(C)lean Message:

Leave your phone at home because we have your back.

A Human Story:

When we first met Sally, she was the VP of Engineering for Acme Corp, and she told us about the time her phone lit up with server issues while she was at her daughter's dance recital. She had to slip out the back of the room to deal with the problem and missed her daughter's big moment on stage. That is a moment she will never get back. After using our solution, she likes to say that she 'feels human again.' Like she can balance the important things in her life, along with her demanding career. Sally is crushing it at work, but more importantly, she knows she will never miss another moment with her family.

Number Stories:

Every time a baby is born in Amsterdam a new startup is founded around the world

Imagine if every time you bought a bunch of bananas, one of them was already brown & squishy. That's what it's like in your office right now. About 1 out of every 7 people in the office are not engaged with their work.

Earworms:

We turn server alerts into lemonade.

We don't sell dashboards. We sell Sundays with your family.

Alerts are for chumps.

(C)lean Messaging

CHAPTER ELEVEN

(C)lean Messaging in Conversation

Once you have your (C)lean Messaging canvas, you are ready to start testing it in real conversation. Fortunately, this is the fun part!

(C)lean Messaging

With the canvas done, you have all the answers you need to most high-level questions about your business. Your only job is to match the right answer to the question being asked.

I wish I could say that the people you will be speaking with really want to know and understand your company or idea. With potential customers or investors, we all hope that there will be a time that your listener wants to get into the weeds and deeply understand what you have built. However, you will never get the chance to have that in-depth conversation until you have crossed the "why should I care?" barrier.

The goal of the (C)lean Messaging framework is to help you get to that deep conversation faster.

When you are talking to the media, it would be great if the interviewer is genuinely interested in your business. However, the sad reality is that they are more interested in how your idea will help them with their audience. Too often the reporter you are speaking with has two big questions running through their head while they are listening to you:

- How can this startup drive interest/action from my audience?
- How can I write about this in a way that drives engagement from my audience?

WHY SHOULD I CARE?

Potential customers or investors are inundated with stories, ideas, and pitches every day. In most of those cases, the person doing the pitch is focused on themselves.

Imagine you are walking down the street, and one hundred people are yelling "LOOK AT ME! LOOK AT ME!". That is the experience of most people today. Our world is full of companies and people who want you to look at them. As the competition for attention increases, those voices get louder.

In this noisy world, our brains have become finely tuned to listen for those voices that illuminate something important. We tune out the noise and listen carefully for some signal.

When we hear that signal, we immediately tune in and try to determine if this signal is important.

Your new (C)lean Messaging canvas is the roadmap to becoming an important signal for listeners in the world.

Your listener's attention is like a castle with three deep and treacherous moats. To get the next conversation, you need to navigate these barriers as quickly as possible.

Attention Moat #1: Is this signal or noise?

To immediately defeat moat #1, we need to separate ourselves from the noise using our earworms & sound bites. That final section of our canvas that has the short, clever & attention-getting phrases that can pull the focus to your story.

We want those earworms to be the headlines and clickable phrases that people read online.

We want those earworms to be the answer to a question like "What are you working on these days?".

We should use those earworms when we introduce ourselves.

We should use those earworms when we want the listener to respond with "wait, what? I gotta hear more about this..."

Once you grab the listeners attention, you have crossed moat #1 and are headed for the next significant barrier.

Attention Moat #2: Is this important?

Once you have crossed the first moat, your listener is trying to determine if what you are talking about is important.   Importance is fickle, but we can always rely on the core human signals of importance. Deep in our reptilian brain, we are all asking if the experience we are having right now will either hurt me or help me.

As we experience the world, our brain is always on the lookout for those things that can harm us and those things that will be a benefit to our long-term survival. Am I in danger? Should I run? Will this thing help me gather resources? Will this help me elevate my status in the tribe?

I like to use a (C)lean Messaging elevator pitch to cross this moat.

Remember, your listener doesn't care about you, they are looking out for their interest at this stage, so we always start with the "Something about Them" section of the canvas. That will hook the listener into the problem or the vision of the opportunity.

Once you have them hooked on the thing about them, you use the (C)lean Message to show them how you will help them solve this problem in their life. This should capture the emotional decision-making center of the brain and get the listener more inclined to agree.

Now, that the listener is inclined to agree we give them some rational reasons to support the decision their emotional brain has already made. We can use the number analogy section of the canvas at this point. This gives the listener the words they can use to describe *why* they agree with you.

Using our (C)lean Messaging canvas, we can feed your listener the data they need to justify and describe your business easily. You can lead your listener through the importance decision by linking sections of your canvas with a few key words. The elevator pitch structure looks like this:

You know how...<Something about Them>

What we do is... <(C)lean Message>

In fact, <Number Story>

This simple structure will focus the listener on a problem they can relate to personally, show how you are helping people just like them with that problem, and then give them some rational data they can use to describe why they agree with you.

Simple and powerful.

If we go back to our canvas for the server company we have been talking about, we can see how it all works together.

Servers, Inc. Elevator Pitch

You know how people just want to disconnect when they leave the office?

What we do is let you leave your phone at home when you go on holiday, because we will have your back.

In fact, every time a baby is born in Amsterdam, another tech startup is founded. That means every month, 148,000 new VPs of Engineering, like you, are going to miss their kid's ballgame or dance recital or lose sleep because we haven't met them yet.

When you get this simple elevator pitch right, the listener should be nodding their head and respond with something like "Cool, tell me more?".

"Tell me more," is your invitation to cross Attention Moat #2. If you can get your listener to feel that they want to learn a little more, you are now on your way to the final attention barrier.

Attention Moat #3: Why should I care?

Why someone should care is the big boss of attention.

If you can cross this barrier, you will have the chance to do a deep dive on your business with the listener.

Now is the time to bring out the story of another person who was in the same position as your listener and share how their life has changed. Your listener is going to listen to the story and picture themselves in the position of the hero, so we want to use this opportunity to show what life is like after a person uses your product.

Remember, your cue that you have reached the Attention Moat #3 is someone inviting you to tell them more.

Listener: *Huh, that's interesting. Tell me more?*

   You: *When we first met Sally, she was the VP of Engineering for Acme Corp, and she told us about the time her phone lit up with server issues while she was at her daughter's dance recital. She had to slip out the back of the room to deal with* *the issue and missed her daughter's big moment on stage. That is a moment she will never get back.*

After using our solution, she likes to say that she 'feels human again.' Like she can balance the important things in her life, along with her demanding career. Sally is crushing it at work, but more importantly, she knows she will never miss another moment with her family.

Sally is just one of many examples of the people we are helping every day. I bet you know someone like Sally?

How will you know that you have indeed crossed the final moat? Your listener will start asking a bunch of questions about *how* you solve this problem or asking for more stories or data. Once that happens, you have now earned your listeners attention, and their permission to start going deep.

Once you have been invited into that castle of attention, you must treat it as sacred. Don't bump into the furniture, and don't break stuff. As you engage in more conversation with the listener, as you prove that you can be trusted with the listener's attention, you are free to ask for a next step.

As a rule of thumb, you should always have an "ask" ready for when you are in this situation. Are you looking for investors? Ask for an introduction. Are you looking for sales? Ask for the deal or ask for a meeting to do a demo of the product.

Don't squander your chance to move the conversation forward.

As you are progressing through the barriers of attention, remember where you are in the process. If your listener tunes out or changes the subject, it is likely that you are not going to get much further in the process. You could try variations of your

(C)lean Messaging

(C)lean Message to get back on the path. Later on, we will talk about the importance of having more than one canvas, but for now, remember that you are always testing these words. So, if it doesn't work, tweak the words and try again with the next person until you find something that will be repeatable.

The final trap you should know about in this process is a tendency to go backward in the process. There is a chance that your listener will "get it" at Attention Moat #1 and jump directly to questions about "the how" of your business. If that happens, you are in the castle of attention, so don't put yourself outside the walls again, by repeating an elevator pitch. Know where you are, and let the listener guide you.

It's about them. Not you.

HOW DOES THIS HELP ME?

Talking with the media is fun if you understand the rules of engagement.

Reporters, bloggers, podcasters, all of these media creators are generating content on behalf of an audience. When you are speaking with a reporter, remember that your message should be focused on their audience, not the reporter. The reporter is the megaphone that will help craft your story for their audience.

If your goal is to get the blogger to write a story about your business, you need to make sure that you are making it easy for them to translate.

The reporter has two key questions they will be thinking about during your conversation:

How can this startup drive interest/action from my audience?

(C)lean Messaging

The good news here is that the way to answer this question is the same as the process for crossing the Attention Moats we discussed earlier.

Contrary to popular belief, most reporters are actually human. They will recognize the same issues and challenges as your potential customers. Often, I have found that writers are great at this; they have a unique ability to put themselves in the position of others and imagine a world where they are the VP of Engineering and struggle with work/life balance.

It is that creative empathy that makes them a great writer.

Use the tools above to help the reporter picture themselves and their audience in the role of the hero, and you will capture their imagination. Your real challenge is the second big question.

How can I write about this in a way that drives engagement from my audience?

The reporter's job is not to just listen to you and then attend another meeting. If the reporter took time to speak with you, they need to create something from this conversation for their audience. Therefore, the writer is going to be thinking about how they turn this conversation into content that will help propel their goals.

In this situation, you will have a leg up.

Content creators are always looking for the same things:

A strong hook to capture the attention of their reader. Leverage a few of your earworms to give the reporter ideas for their headline or hook. The easier you make it, the more likely they will be to write a great story and invite you back for another.

(C)lean Messaging

A clear value for their audience.   By using your (C)lean Message, it will be simple and obvious the value you are bringing to the writer's audience.

A great human story.   Writers love stories.   Go figure.

When you are speaking with the media, make it easy for them to pull your story into the sections they need to make a compelling piece of content.

CHAPTER TWELVE
You Need More Than One

Building your first (C)lean Messaging canvas is usually the hardest. I always recommend starting with a broad view of the company or top-level idea first. However, having one canvas is usually not enough.

(C)lean Messaging

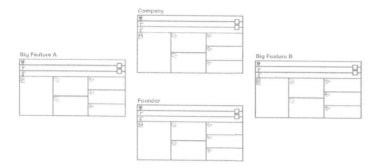

Once you have the company (C)lean Messaging canvas completed, pick one or two of the essential features of your product or business and do a separate canvas for those features.

You may decide to do a canvas for each of the significant customer types in your business. For example, if you were running the search division at Google, you might decide to do a (C)lean Messaging canvas for search users and another one for search advertisers.

If your business has "customers" with very different profiles or distinct "deep human needs" that would make the first section of "Something About Them" unique, that is a pretty strong sign that you need multiple canvases.

Once you have the company, and a couple of significant product features, you may consider doing a canvas for each of the principal founders of the company. Having multiple (C)lean Messaging canvases will give you ample content to use during media interviews. It will give you key messages to talk about the background of each founder, and why they are uniquely able to change the world with their business.

When you have four canvases finished, you will have a minimum of four strong (C)lean Messaging canvases that will be the foundation for how you talk to humans. This will result in:

- Four strong (C)lean Messages

- Four great human stories
- Eight number stories that people will remember
- Twelve "earworms" that people will share and turn into headlines

From that foundation, you have all the material you need to do amazing interviews, sell product and raise venture capital.

CHAPTER THIRTEEN
Startup Examples

(C)lean Messaging has been used by hundreds of startups to help craft their message. The results have been amazing.

We see shorter average times in fundraising, shorter sales cycles, and excellent media coverage. All of these outcomes make a material difference in the likelihood of success for a startup.

I've included a few examples from some of my favorite startups, along with a bit of commentary on what works and what could be stronger.

AVERON

Averon provides secure, frictionless authentication. I like to think of them as doing two-factor authentication, without the hassle of the second factor.

You know those times when you sign into your bank, and they send you an SMS message to validate your login? Averon has worked with mobile operators to use the fact that you are connected to the internet using your identified network connection to vouch for the second factor for authentication.

This unique capability allows people like us to get a more secure login without the hassle. Cool, right? You can learn more about Averon at https://www.averon.com

Let's have a look at their (C)lean Message canvas:

Something About Them:

Logins are broken. We fix that, enabling a secure zero-tap login experience that increases conversion rates.

My friends at Averon snuck a little bit about themselves into a section that should be all about the listener. I think if they would have stopped with the simple statement that "Logins are broken," we would all agree with them. In fact, it is a problem that so many of us feel innately, that it stands on its own. The challenge for them may be in understanding the true identity of their listener. Is it random people in the world who log in to things, or the companies that provide the internet connection? Their listener could even be the company that people are logging in to in this canvas. If the listener is the provider or the website company, I might suggest another look at the deeper human need.

Something About You:

We use signaling inherent in Internet networks to deliver seamless, secure authentication solutions.

Right on. It is clear, simple, and straight to the point. Still sounds a little like "science" for a non-technical listener, but that is to be expected in this section. In the next part, we will see how they take these first two parts and combine them into a strong (C)lean Message.

(C)lean Message:

Averon enables you to deliver delightful zero-tap logins which drive user engagement

Such a cool idea. It looks like we have our answer to whom Averon thinks the listener is for this canvas. From my reading, it appears the "you" they are speaking with is either a service provider or website company. If the value they are bringing is to "drive user engagement," they are clearly not speaking with a random human. We know that a good (C)lean Message starts with the listener. In this example, Averon is starting with themselves. So, let's flip it.

"Drive increased user engagement with delightful zero-tap logins using Averon."

That's better, but I still get hung up on the phrase "zero-tap logins." I might ask them to test a few other phrases with customers to find one that is more emotionally compelling. "Zero-tap" doesn't feel like a big enough benefit, if my alternative is a "one-tap" login.

A Human Story:

When our CEO Wendell Brown was trying to make a payment through an app, he couldn't: he was stuck in a seemingly endless password reset process.

(C)lean Messaging

Later, he took his phone out of his pocket to make a call. He noted that to do so he didn't need to log in to anything - his mobile carrier already knew who he was - they had to as they were going to send him a bill for the call at the end of the month (guaranteed).

He thought to himself, "Why don't the apps on my phone know who I am?". He decided to join the dots, and that's what Averon does, by making the identity signals in networks available to companies wanting to secure and ease user logins.

This is a strong origin story for the business. Averon should use this on a (C)lean Messaging canvas they build for Wendell. When the listener is a potential service provider, this story may help to underscore the problem, but it will be less likely to help propel the buying decision forward. The listener will hear this story and imagine themselves inventing the solution. What they won't do, is imagine themselves deploying the solution to great acclaim.

Two Number Stories:

First: The average person has 25 accounts, logs into 8 accounts each day, and reuses the same ~6 passwords across sites.

First Analogy: All told, people worldwide spend more than 1,000 years each day logging in to systems using the same few passwords, drastically increasing their risk exposure.

Nearly Perfect.   You can imagine this in the lead paragraph of the blog post, right?   The only way I would improve this is to simplify the language. They could try changing "drastically increasing their risk exposure," to "increasing their chances of being hacked."

Second: 87% of consumers landing on an e-commerce mobile site will leave without executing a transaction.

Second Analogy: Using the Internet today is like walking down Main Street in your hometown, but all the stores are locked, and you have a keychain with dozens of keys on there. You have to remember which key (which password) to use if you even want to browse the site.

Another good number story from Averon. Hearing this, you can feel the weight of that big keychain. It clearly aligns the weight of all those keys with the frustration and abandonment of the e-commerce site.

Three Earworms:

Averon is creating a new standard for digital identity. As a Fortune 500 CEO said about us, "This is an idea whose time has come."

We save the average person 8 hours per year by eliminating authentication hurdles.

Only 36% of app downloads result in a registered user. In this age of distraction, we need zero-tap logins.

Our friends from Averon may need to work harder on this section. Their second earworm, "We save the average person 8 hours per year...", is good. However, the other two will be tough on the listener. Averon has a lot to brag about, but they might consider a few earworms that are more focused on the listener's experience when logging into a website, rather than what people think about their company. Alternatively, they could find an earworm that will connect more directly with the pain felt by the website owner.

BLITZZ

Blitzz has built some technology that helps large service providers fix problems once and eliminate the need for repeat service calls.

You know those times when you need someone to come out to your house to fix a problem with your internet connection, and it turns out they can't fix it on that first trip? Incredibly frustrating for people, right? Well, with Blitzz you would be able to do a real-time video call with the service provider that could allow them to fix the problem without even having to send a person.

Even better, when the field technician is on-site, they can use augmented reality glasses to leverage all the smart people back at the office to make sure they fix the problem once and don't have to request a second visit. You can learn more about Blitzz at https://blitzz.co

Let's take a look at their version of a (C)lean Messaging canvas:

Something About Them:

Field techs want to get their jobs done right the first time and go back to their families at the end of the day feeling rewarded, appreciated, and their bonus paid out - instead of feeling embarrassed or dinged for a job not done.

I agree with this. Maybe Blitzz could simplify it with: "People want to do a good job and feel bad when that doesn't happen." Depending on the audience he might swap 'people' for a more specific term like field tech, customer service rep, or the guy that comes to your house to fix your broadband connection.

Something About You:
We have built a video collaboration platform using AR and AI to help field techs collaborate with end users, other field techs, and customer service teams.

Again, this is usually the easy one for most companies doing their (C)lean Messaging canvas for the first time. All you need to do is put down the simplest explanation of what you do. In this case, it is very clear.

(C)lean Message:

We empower field techs to get their jobs done, by being a force multiplier of the 'smart people' in their company.

Very strong (C)lean Message. They lead with the listener's problem and then follow up with how they can help. I like the idea of being a force multiplier of 'smart people.' They could also try something along the lines of: "Every field tech can be as great as your best field tech with Blitzz."

A Human Story:

A few months ago, when we did a ride along with Dmitry, a field tech at OperatorX. We saw him struggle to complete jobs, as he got stuck with technical issues that he had not encountered before and had to reschedule the job because he couldn't reach any expert to have eyes on the problem and walk him through the solution step-by-step. Today with Blitzz, he has smart people help him over live video and access to a cloud-based video repository at his fingertips.   He powers through the trickiest of jobs and even has Blitzz's AI engine recommend tech tips & videos to watch specifically for the next job at hand.

You can see that Blitzz is really trying to tell a human story here.   They share where Dmitry was struggling, and how he is better off now that he has their product. I would suggest that Blitzz try to raise the stakes a bit in this story.   When Dmitry had to reschedule what was the impact on him and his family?   Did he miss his bonus because this was happening all too often?   If they push a little closer to the human struggle, they may find that the story will better resonate with the listener.

Two Number Stories:

(C)lean Messaging

First: 52% of jobs don't get done right the first time.

First Analogy: Getting a job done right the first time is a coin toss!

Yes! Love this one. Imagining that you are only going to get a job done right the first time based on a coin flip is beyond troubling. The listener will immediately feel like this problem is real and deserves to be fixed.

Second: 33% percent of trucks sent out to a customer are avoidable.

Second Analogy: If we stacked all the trucks that were rolled out unnecessarily in any given year, they would easily overshoot the international space station which orbits the earth at the height of 254 miles!

The Blitzz team is doing great with their number stories. I would suggest they play with the language a bit to make it easier on the ear, but the content is strong. This is an example of what we discussed about being "ear-worthy." When you say these words out loud, it just doesn't sound right. Looking for the poetry in this, you might say: "If we stacked up all the bucket trucks that were sent for no reason this year, you could climb those ladders all the way to the space station." At least to my ear, this sounds better. Remember that "ear worthy" is subjective, but we all know it when we hear it.

Three Earworms:

Every truck roll should be one-and-done

Have your smartest people ride along with every field tech

We are manifesting the omniscient super tech!

This Blitzz team is on a roll! Truck roll's being 'one-and-done' is great. Very easy to remember and will be the thing that the listener repeats to their friends. I like the idea that all your smart people can ride along with every field tech, as well. Many smart people in a truck is a strong visual that will make an impression on the listener.

Let's talk about "manifesting the omniscient super tech." I am torn on this one. I can envision an audience that would love it, and if you met the Blitzz team, it makes perfect sense that they would write this down. For me, I would keep this in the list, but only use it when I am in a room of experienced field techs or their leadership. It's an "inside baseball" statement that will do well with the right audience and be a total dud in a different context.

MUTABLE

We have all felt the power and simplicity of cloud computing. The challenge is that for some interesting use cases, the problem is not getting access to the compute resources, the problem is latency.

Meet Mutable. Mutable is turning the data centers that exist within 25 miles of every house in North America, and operated by mobile, telco and broadband providers, into a new public edge cloud that is perfect for those ultra-low latency use cases.

Applications that could benefit from this new low latency solution include gaming companies, DNS, IoT, advertising technologies, and many others. As you will see in their canvas below, Mutable believes that latency is the new bandwidth. Learn more at http://mutable.io

Let's look at their (C)lean Messaging canvas:

Something About Them:

(C)lean Messaging

Broadband operators are looking for new revenue streams [that tap into subscriber needs/ desires for faster services, better experience, and richer content]

A great way to start. Their customers are broadband operators that are in search of new revenue, and from their research, it looks like new revenue is a strong motivation. I wonder if it is 'human' enough to move the needle for their buyers. One way to tweak this might be to make it more personal to the actual buyer in the room.

Something About You:
We have a platform for low latency edge compute

Simple and true. Nothing to add here. Well done.

(C)lean Message:
We turn edge compute real estate into passive new revenue for MSOs

Scott Brown

I like where this is going, but I would suggest reversing the points. Lead with the need, then follow up with the answer. Perhaps something like: "You can make new passive revenue from your network edge real estate with Mutable." This puts the focus on the listener in a stronger way.

A Human Story:

Imagine: Simply by providing Mutable access to their headends, OperatorX is able to add a new business service line, OperatorX Cloud.

This story is weak, in my view. The Mutable team could do a better job here by talking about what life is like now for the person that approved a Mutable deal. An actual person approved their deal at OperatorX, so what happened to that person, now that they are getting a steady passive revenue stream? Did they get promoted? Were they surprised by the income? Are they a hero in the company?

Two Number Stories:

First: 4,000 operator headends vs. 18 public cloud locations

First Analogy: For every one public cloud, there are 222 operator owned headend data centers

This number story is interesting and certainly sets the context for the listener. Having 200x the locations is a big deal. This number story is likely to resonate in a sales call, but may fall flat in the press, because very few people in the world know what they mean by a 'headend data center.' If they are talking to the media, they should either define the 'headend' early in the conversation or use simplified language to describe it.

Second: Public cloud infrastructure is 1000 miles away; operator headend is 25 miles away. 40x closer

Second Analogy: the public cloud distance can be further away from their customer than the length of the state of California, while the Mutable cloud would be closer to their home than the length of the city of Los Angeles

Another statistic story related to the number of data centers and their distance to the home. Mutable might get better traction by focusing on the number of actual people that can feel the benefit of this new low latency edge compute. They would get the same result by talking to the effect that low latency services could have on gaming, IoT, or web page load times.

Three Earworms:

New passive revenue for broadband operators.

Your edge is your advantage.

Latency is the new bandwidth.

(C)lean Messaging

Wahoo! These are great. You can see a few of them as headlines, and they are punchy enough that a person will ask for more information after them.

CHAPTER FOURTEEN
Conclusion

(C)lean Messaging is a framework to help startup founders, like you, talk to people about the amazing things they have built.   To build a successful company is pretty simple. You need to build something people want to buy and sell it for more than it costs to make.   Then repeat that strategy over and over again.

With modern startup tools and frameworks, it is not hard to figure out what to build or even who to build it for; the challenge is in capturing the attention of all those people in a world who are overwhelmed with people shouting for focus.

(C)lean Messaging

Using this framework, you can be the signal in this noisy world.

None of us launch a startup knowing that there are no potential buyers for our product. And yet, 42% of founders look back at their startup failures and say they could never find a market for their product. With (C)lean Messaging you can change that dynamic. Once you have built a business, it's not about market fit; it's about market framing.

The (C)lean Messaging framework starts with a focus on the listener. Who needs to hear your story, and what is the most profound human need or desire that the listener is holding? Identify that deep human element, and you will be able to tap into the emotional decision maker in the human brain.

When you get out of the office and start talking to people about your new company, please remember that it is no longer about you. No one cares what you have built; people care about how what you have built will help them.

It's about the listener, not you.

As technical startup founders, this process will feel unnatural at first. At some point, you will find yourself pounding the desk and wondering why you are spending time working on this canvas when there is code to be written. I challenge you to push through and do the work. There is no truth to the old crutch that "if you build it they will come."

If you build it, no one cares.

Once you have built something that a *few people* care about, it is time to lean into the (C)lean Messaging work and frame your idea as something that *the world* will notice. What will life be like for you when people understand your idea and the revolution you are starting in the first twenty seconds? What will life be like for your customers?

What if your message was as clean as your code?

You can download the (C)lean Messaging framework by visiting:

http://CleanMessaging.co/canvas

Please remember to sign up for the (C)lean Messaging newsletter, to get updates and hear stories of other startup founders using this framework to grow their business. I promise never to sell or share your information and will respect your communication preferences.

To see what others are doing with (C)lean Messaging, search Twitter for the hashtag #cleanmessaging and join the conversation. If you post your (C)lean Message to Twitter with the hashtag #cleanmessaging, I will try to comment and pass along a few ideas.

If you found this little book helpful in the process of crafting a (C)lean Messaging that will help you close deals faster, please leave a review on Amazon and let others know. Together, we are on a mission to help startup founders talk to humans.

Thank you!

CHAPTER FIFTEEN

About the Author

Scott Brown has been a long-time technologist and entrepreneur with a strong history of building companies from inception to profitability. Currently, he is the Chief Executive Officer for Immersion Neuroscience - a software platform that allows anyone to measure the way a persons brain truly values content and predict market outcomes. Backed by 20 years of research, Immersion has been proven to predict hits for TV, movies, and music with over 80% accuracy. In fact, Scott has used this predictive power of neuroscience to measure startup messaging and investment pitches for many leading companies.

As an active angel investor and advisor, Scott has helped hundreds of startups perfect their pitch with a framework he created called (C)lean Messaging.

As a speaker, Scott has been invited to share his insight with audiences around the world on the topics of innovation, startups, messaging and sales. You will often find Scott on the road having beer or coffee with startup founders and helping them find the heart of their story.

In 2016, Scott is credited with inventing the worlds' first bacon-wrapped tot.

Connect with Scott:

https://scottbrown.co/

https://twitter.com/sbrown

https://www.linkedin.com/in/sc0ttbr0wn/

https://medium.com/@stbrown

https://www.GetImmersion.com

Made in the USA
Monee, IL
24 February 2020